D1084373

Hindsight

Hindsight

The Promise and Peril
of Looking Backward

Mark Freeman

OXFORD
UNIVERSITY PRESS

2010

OXFORD
UNIVERSITY PRESS

Oxford University Press, Inc., publishes works that further
Oxford University's objective of excellence
in research, scholarship, and education.

Oxford   New York
Auckland   Cape Town   Dar es Salaam   Hong Kong   Karachi
Kuala Lumpur   Madrid   Melbourne   Mexico City   Nairobi
New Delhi   Shanghai   Taipei   Toronto

With offices in
Argentina   Austria   Brazil   Chile   Czech Republic   France   Greece
Guatemala   Hungary   Italy   Japan   Poland   Portugal   Singapore
South Korea   Switzerland   Thailand   Turkey   Ukraine   Vietnam

Copyright © 2010 by Oxford University Press

Published by Oxford University Press, Inc.
198 Madison Avenue, New York, New York 10016

www.oup.com

Oxford is a registered trademark of Oxford University Press

Library of Congress Cataloging-in-Publication Data

Freeman, Mark Philip, 1955–
Hindsight : the promise and peril of looking backward / Mark Freeman. — 1st ed.
p. cm.
Includes bibliographical references and index.
ISBN 978-0-19-538993-7
1. Hindsight bias (Psychology) I. Title.
BF378.H54.F74 2009
153—dc22
2009030184

1 3 5 7 9 8 6 4 2

Printed in the United States of America
on acid-free paper

To Deborah, Brenna, Justine, and my mother, Marian,
in recognition of the lives and love we share

We will not know the worth of water 'til the well is dry.

—Chinese fortune cookie

What would I give
To start all over again
To clean up my mistakes?

—Tom Petty, "Only a Broken Heart"
From *Wildflowers* (1994)

ACKNOWLEDGMENTS

During the course of writing this book, along with the many other writing projects that have led up to it, I have benefited greatly from the work, wisdom, and counsel of numerous fellow travelers in the various arenas of thought explored herein. These include, among many others, Molly Andrews, Michael Bamberg, Art Bochner, Jacob Belzen, Jens Brockmeier, Jerome Bruner, Bert Cohler, Peter Coleman, Matti Hyvärinen, Ruthellen Josselson, Suzanne Kirschner, Amia Lieblich, Jack Martin, Dan McAdams, Katherine Nelson, Bill Randall, Jeff Sugarman, and Harald Welzer. Some of these people I know personally a good deal better than others; some, in fact, have become good friends. With all, however, there has been a spirit of vital intellectual exchange and camaraderie that I have cherished. Thank you.

I also want to acknowledge several intellectual communities that I have had the great good fortune of being a part of while writing this book. These include the one comprised of friends and colleagues from Holy Cross, especially Bob Cording, Chris Dustin, Margaret Freije, Jim Kee, Vicki Swigert, Steve Vineberg, Chick Weiss, and Jody Ziegler, along with my fellow readers from the Philosophy Reading Group, all of whom, at some point or other, were subjected to my musings if not my latest tomes; the Narrative Study Group, coordinated and sponsored graciously for many years by Elliot Mishler, including especially Susan Bell, Arlene Katz, Kristin Langellier, Brinton Lykes, Eric Peterson, Cathy Riessman, Ellen Rintell, and Jill Taylor; and, most recently, the Society for Personology, a group of scholars strenuously committed to studying human lives in all of their complexity and richness.

Finally, I want to recognize two individuals, now gone, whose work and spirit pervade much of what I have thought and written about through the years: Bernard Kaplan, who was the G. Stanley Hall Professor of genetic psychology at Clark University, and Paul Ricoeur, who was the John Nuveen Professor in the divinity school as well as professor of philosophy and social thought at the University of Chicago. Although I never took a class with Bernie, he served for many years as teacher, provocateur, conversation partner, and, not least, friend. He will be sorely missed. As for Paul Ricoeur, it still strikes me now as a matter of sheer luck that I landed at the University of Chicago at the very period when he was teaching and writing about time, memory, narrative, identity, and other such notions that have come to be at the very heart of what I do and indeed who I am. I did, of course, know and feel "all along" the influence of the many individuals just named. But this very influence, far from being limited to the moment, continues to deepen over time, as I look backward and try to discern, and discern again, the formative roles they have played in my life and work. I am extremely grateful to them all.

I am also grateful to the College of the Holy Cross, for having not only let me do what I do, as a teacher and writer, for 20-plus years but for providing an usually hospitable and fertile environment for pursuing those "basic human questions" (as the

College's Mission Statement puts it) that are central both to liberal arts education and to human existence itself.

Last but not least, this book is a product of the efforts of a number of individuals at Oxford University Press, including Catharine Carlin, Mallory Jensen, and Marion Osmun. I am grateful to them too, and thank them for their support for the project, their helpful commentary, and for their hard work helping to bring it into its current form.

It should be noted that *Hindsight* represents a synthesis of much of the work I have done over the course of the last 15 or so years. Although none of the chapters found here reproduces in full work that has been published elsewhere, a number of them do in fact make significant contact with this earlier work. Articles and chapters drawn upon include "Death, narrative integrity, and the radical challenge of self-understanding: A reading of Tolstoy's *Death of Ivan Ilych,*" *Ageing and Society,* 1997, *17,* 373–398; "Mythical time, historical time, and the narrative fabric of the self," *Narrative Inquiry,* 1998, *8,* 27–50; "When the story's over: Narrative foreclosure and the possibility of self-renewal," in M. Andrews, S.D. Sclater, C. Squire, & A. Treacher (Eds.), *Lines of Narrative: Psychosocial Perspectives,* pp. 81–91 (London: Routledge, 2000); "The presence of what is missing: Memory, poetry, and the ride home," in R.J. Pellegrini & T.R. Sarbin (Eds.), *Between Fathers and Sons: Critical Incident Narratives in the Development of Men's Lives,* pp. 165–176 (Binghamton, NY: Haworth, 2002); "Charting the narrative unconscious: Cultural memory and the challenge of autobiography," *Narrative Inquiry,* 2002, *12,* 193–211; "Too late: The temporality of memory and the challenge of moral life," *Journal für Psychologie,* 2003, *11,* 54–74; "Rethinking the fictive, reclaiming the real: Autobiography, narrative time, and the burden of truth," in

G. Fireman, T. McVay, & O. Flanagan (Eds.), *Narrative and Consciousness: Literature, Psychology, and the Brain,* pp. 115–128 (New York: Oxford University Press, 2003).

Grateful acknowledgment is made to the following for permission to reprint copyrighted material. Emily Fox Gordon: excerpts from "Book of Days" (*The American Scholar*, Vol. 72, No. 1, Winter 2003). Eva Hoffman: *After Such Knowledge: History, Memory, and the Legacy of the Holocaust.* New York: Perseus Books Group, 2004; reprinted with permission. Primo Levi: *The Drowned and the Saved.* New York: The Penguin Group, 1989; reprinted with permission. *Leo Tolstoy: The Death of Ivan Ilych and Other Stories* (trans. by Aylmer Maude and J.D. Duff). New York: Signet Classics, 1960; reprinted by permission of Oxford University Press.

CONTENTS

Seven

Coda

Hindsight

INTRODUCTION: THE POWER
OF HINDSIGHT

This book grows out of an obsession that has been with me for more than two decades, and it has to do with the relationship between life as lived, moment to moment, and life as told, in retrospect, from the vantage point of the present—between what essayist Sven Birkerts, in his recent (2008) book *The Art of Time in Memoir,* refers to as the "then" of past experience and the "again" in which experience is revisited at some subsequent point in time. "Memoir," Birkerts writes, "begins not with the event but with the intuition of meaning—with the mysterious fact that life can some-times step free from the chaos and contingency and become story" (pp. 3–4). This does not mean that events are irrelevant. Indeed, one of the challenges of writing a memoir is precisely to hold in tension both then and now, past and present, "to discover the nonsequential connections that allow [past] experiences to make larger sense" and to show the way in which "circumstance becomes meaningful when seen from a certain remove" (p. 4). I shall have a good deal more to say about memoir in the chapters to follow.

My primary concern in this book, however, is not memoir but the movement of life itself. The fact is, everything just said about memoir can be extended to the ongoing process of living, with its endless parade of present moments and its reflective pauses, its takings-stock. All of this is happening right now, as I write these very words: I move forward into the future, moment following moment, and then pause to see what's been said, armed now with that measure of distance that might allow me to see things a bit more clearly. I survey and reflect, and perhaps revise, in order to continue on more surely. But I am after bigger issues in this book than these more momentary circumstances. For my primary concern here, ultimately, is nothing less than the project of self-understanding, which, I argue, has hindsight at its very core. In speaking of hindsight, therefore, I am referring specifically to the process of looking back over the terrain of the past from the standpoint of the present and either seeing things anew or drawing "connections," as Birkerts had put it, that could not possibly be drawn during the course of ongoing moments but only in retrospect. What this suggests, in turn, is that hindsight is not only about *memory* but about *narrative;* and this is so, I would add, whether or not one takes the time to tell the story of one's life. When I look backward over the course of some portion of my life in order to discern possible connections, I am inevitably engaging in narrative "emplotment," the experiences of times past now being seen as parts of an emerging whole, episodes in an evolving story.[1] Hence the first part of my two-fold thesis: *Self-understanding occurs, in significant part, through narrative reflection, which is itself a product of hindsight.*

---

[1] The work of the philosopher Paul Ricoeur looms large throughout the pages of this book. See especially his monumental three-volume *Time and Narrative*, 1984, 1985, 1988; see also 1981, 1991. On the issue of emplotment, see also White, 1978, 1990. For important works of "narrative psychology," see especially Bruner, 1990, 2003; Polkinghorne, 1988; Sarbin, 1986. See also the bibliographic note following the coda of this book.

But there is another aspect of hindsight that needs to be emphasized as well, having to do with our tendency to get caught up in the moment, to act first and think later. "How *could* I?" we ask. "What was I *thinking?*" "If only . . . . " These are the sorts of moments we want back, only to arrive at the harsh and terrible realization that they are gone, forever. This can be especially troubling in the sphere of moral life. Looking backward, we can frequently see things that we could not, or would not, see earlier on. And it can be painful, indeed. I can think of many, many things that have happened during the course of my life that look very different in hindsight than they did at the moment they occurred. In the heat of the moment, I can be utterly certain about the truth of the matter or utterly sure about the validity of my position—and, of course, the *in*validity of yours. I can be convinced that I had no choice whatsoever but to act the way I did. But then, after the moment passes, I see it all differently. I have gained some perspective, and so, what had seemed at the time to be unequivocally true or right turns out to have been quite false or wrong. Through hindsight I have not only achieved a measure of insight, I have taken a step, however small, in the direction of moral growth. By "moral," I refer not only to those specific spheres of experience frequently associated with "good" and "bad" behavior (i.e., "morality"), but also to those broader spheres of experience (frequently considered under the rubric of "ethics") that have to do with fundamental questions about how to live. Hence, the second part of my thesis: *hindsight plays an integral role in shaping and deepening moral life.*

It may strike some readers as strange that hindsight should be accorded the profound significance for knowing and being that it is being accorded here. The word "hindsight," in psychology, is most often followed by the word "bias," the widely held presumption being that hindsight is most appropriately regarded as a source of distortion of "what really was." Especially pernicious is the much-maligned "20/20" hindsight, the tendency to proclaim, after the fact, that "I knew it all along."[2] There is no question that hindsight bias is quite real and that it can result in bad history; that is, in portraits of the past that confer illusory significance or prominence on certain events. So it is that hindsight has gotten something of a bad name in the psychological literature. Beyond the discipline of psychology, particularly in the context of meditative or "mindfulness" practices and the like, it is assumed that many of us, chronically preoccupied and inattentive to the world as we may be, need to focus more on the present, the *now*. To take but one notable instance of this idea, consider Eckhart Tolle's bestselling *The Power of Now* (2004), an Oprah Winfrey book club selection that no doubt has millions of people happily ensconced in the present at this very moment. What place could a book that is focused on interpreting the past and that uses words like "remove" and "distance" have in a world increasingly enchanted by the here and now?

I have no interest whatsoever in denying the power of now. Tolle's book is part of a long lineage of works that underscore in a vitally important way both the challenges and the spiritual rewards of being attentive to the present moment. Some of these works also underscore the potential pitfalls of narrative reflection. We can become prisoners of our stories, locked in a world of our own narrative designs, and this sometimes precludes the very possibility of being here, now (see especially Crispin Sartwell's [2000] *End of Story* for the narrative-as-prison thesis).

[2] See, e.g., Hawkins & Hastie, 1990.

We can dwell in the past, returning to and replaying it again and again, somehow imagining that one of these times we will find release. "Let go of your story," the teacher would urge the class I attended on mindfulness. "Let your thoughts float by, like clouds. Just observe what's there, right in front of you. And don't criticize or condemn it or try to make it better. It is what it is." Indeed. I liked the class and benefited from it a great deal. But none of what was said there, or in Tolle or Sartwell or the great traditions of Eastern thought, render the work of hindsight any less important. There is ample room in the human condition for honoring both the power of now and the power of hindsight.

They are not so far apart as they may initially appear either. The dimension of distance is operative in both, involving a process of "separating" oneself from a condition of being enmeshed, caught-up-in. I can be so caught up in the attractions of the moment that I can be blind to the bigger picture, and I can be so preoccupied with this or that nagging thought or wish or regret that I can be blind to what's right in front of me. This suggests yet another significant point of common ground between the power of now and the power of hindsight— namely, that they are both recollective practices that seek to redress the *forgetfulness* that so often characterizes the human condition. They are about *pausing* to attend, whether to past or present; they are about moving from unconsciousness to consciousness; and, not least, they are about living better, more expansively, and with greater awareness of what is real and true.

I don't want to make hindsight sound any more grand than it is. It can be, and frequently is, a source of distortion. It can also be a self-serving and self-protective source of illusion, yielding up consoling fictions for those in need. And as Sartwell, in particular, reminds us, it can result in our building narrative prisons, self-fashioned self-enclosures that are so focused on *telling* that they get in the way of *living*. Nevertheless, hindsight remains *the* primary source of the examined life. And while the examined life in no way guarantees its goodness, it surely ups the chances.

THE PLAN OF THE BOOK

In Chapter 1, "Hindsight, Narrative, and Moral Life," I present some telling examples of hindsight from both life and literature, develop some of the central themes introduced herein, and provide a historical sketch of how this interwoven trio of ideas came to acquire the significance it has. At a most basic level, hindsight is to be considered a vehicle of narrative reflection, binding together the disparate episodes of our lives into story. Important though "the facts of the matter" or "what really happened" may be, they are of a different order than the narrative order. Neither, I maintain, is any more real or true than the other; the fact is, we live in both, shifting between them in line with the demands of our lives. As I have suggested already, hindsight may also be seen as a response, indeed a counterweight, to our pervasive tendency to get "caught up in the moment," to act out of a mindless impulsiveness that too often ends in disaster. Because this tendency is especially pervasive in the moral domain, hindsight frequently serves the role of moral recuperation, of redressing one's "shortsightedness." Natural though this process of looking backward over the terrain of the personal past may seem to us moderns, it has a history. By sketching out the contours of this history, I try to locate the emergence not only of hindsight but also of those very forms of personhood that require it in the service of self-scrutiny and self-knowledge.

In Chapter 2, "The Narrative Imagination," I take the liberty of engaging in some autobiographical reflection of my own in order to highlight the temporal logic of narrative and to show how narrative understanding works. I focus on two distinct scenes in this chapter, one involving my father shortly before his death and the other involving my daughter, who had taken ill with pneumonia a few days before I was to leave town for a conference (on narrative, no less). In considering the first scene, I am most interested in exploring how it is that an ordinary event, one that may have possessed only minimal meaning at the time, comes to be infused with meaning later on, as subsequent events retroactively transfigure it. From one angle, this sort of after-the-fact infusion of meaning may be seen as distortion, the falsification of the past "as it was." From the angle I wish to pursue, however, this reconstructive process—poetic in its essence—can, and should, be understood differently: this simple event, so ordinary in its way, was to become an episode in an all-too-tragic story, a prelude to the end; and in becoming so, it has acquired a kind of mythic status, serving as a monument to the story of a relationship, between my father and me.

The second scene is rather different. At the time of the event's occurrence, it was filled with meaning and significance, but of an open sort: having no idea whatsoever how the story would end—whether my daughter would return to health or plunge more deeply into illness—it was infused with fear and the anxiety of uncertainty, indeterminateness. A story on the news about a young girl, close to my daughter's age, who had died suddenly from pneumonia, heightened my apprehensions, such that I would eventually raise the possibility of there being a connection, an important connection, between my father's death and the experience of my daughter's illness on the eve of my departure. In pondering this connection, I explore how narrative reflection, emerging in and through hindsight, is the key player in this connective process—which, again, is about nothing less than the possibility of self-understanding.

My takeoff point in Chapter 3, "Moral Lateness," is an autobiographical essay by Primo Levi called "Shame," from his book *The Drowned and the Saved* (1989). On one level, his story is a familiar one; like many others who survived the Holocaust, he is saddled with shame and guilt over this very survival. But through one seemingly minor incident at Auschwitz—in which he, along with a fellow prisoner, had greedily gulped down some water they had discovered during the course of an assignment—Levi explores in painful detail the horror of his having succumbed to a level of selfish barbarity that, in his eyes, was all too reminiscent of the barbarity that had been inflicted on him by his captors. It is in this chapter, especially, that we will explore the idea of the human condition as characterized by a certain "lateness." On the spur of the moment, Levi had acted in a manner that had no doubt seemed forgivable, if not entirely justifiable, at the time. But it wasn't too long after that he would look back on this simple act and find in it an emblem of his sinfulness as a human being. He had rediscovered his moral compass and could see what he had been unable, or unwilling, to see at the time. Far from being a source of consolation, however, it was just the opposite, a source of deep and seemingly immovable shame. I therefore ask: What would it take, what *does* it take, to forgive oneself for one's sins? What does it take to free oneself, if only partially, from the dead weight of the past?

Chapter 4, on "The Narrative Unconscious," also begins with an autobiographical scene, my first visit to Berlin some years ago during which, while exploring the city, I suddenly and inexplicably found myself overwhelmed by a mixture of horror, disbelief, and sorrow somehow tied to the city's brutal past.

I hadn't actually known much about the city. Nor did I personally know anyone who had perished under Hitler's awful rule. All I could surmise, via hindsight, was that somehow what I *did* know about the city and the Nazi regime had coalesced into an image of the past whose "undercurrents" had apparently been activated by the spectacles I had observed during my visit.

It was in the wake of this event that I began to entertain the notion of the *narrative unconscious,* which, in broad outline, refers to those culturally rooted aspects of one's history that have yet to become an explicit part of one's story. It was also through this event that I began to think of hindsight as an arena of quite extraordinary complexity. Looking backward, over the terrain of one's life, one needs to take heed not only of what one knows, firsthand, about the past but also of what one has inherited from outside sources, including other people and, as significantly, from the vast array of media—documentary footage, movies, plays, television shows, fantasies, and more—that *mediate* our relationship to the past. I probe this "inheritance" further by examining several texts, among them Eva Hoffman's *After Such Knowledge: Memory, History, and the Legacy of the Holocaust* (2004). Hoffman, the daughter of Holocaust survivors, is a member of what has come to be known as the "second generation," the generation in which received knowledge has become transmuted into story. So it is that she "began discerning, amidst other threads, the Holocaust strand of [her] history. I had carried this part of my psychic past within me all my life," she writes, "but it was only now, as I began pondering it from a longer distance and through the clarifying process of writing, that what had been an inchoate, obscure knowledge appeared to me as a powerful theme and influence in my life" (p. x). What she has to say about the influence of this transferred knowledge upon her own life tells us much about the phenomenon of hindsight. Far from being limited to those events one experiences firsthand, it makes extensive use of outside sources as well. Are these outside sources to be considered part of "memory"? Given the inevitable commingling of first- and secondhand sources, it may be that we need to rethink the very term. In a related vein, what we will also see in this chapter is that "my life," rather than being limited to the discrete events that comprise my past, moves well beyond them, into the very fabric of culture and history.

Chapter 5, "Narrative Foreclosure," tells the story of two artists who each faced a major crisis in their careers. One, a man in his 60s, had become convinced that it was unlikely that he would ever hit his stride as an artist. He was past his prime, or so he thought, with the result that he could not imagine his future as anything other than a bleak repetition of his failures and disappointments. Narrative foreclosure is therefore about the conviction that one's story is effectively over, that no prospect exists for opening up a new chapter. This phenomenon, I suggest, is a widespread one in contemporary Western culture, where growing old is so readily associated with the end of meaningful, productive activity. As will become clear, there is little doubt but that this man had internalized certain aspects of this cultural narrative, as well as the additional narrative of the struggling artist, striving for greatness, working against the odds, unable fully to measure up to the god-like being he had imagined he might someday become. The challenge, in cases such as this one, is to identify the ways in which these cultural narratives have permeated one's being and, in the process, to break away from them and sap them of their coercive power. This, of course, is easier said than done; it is no simple matter to "restart" a story that feels like it has ended. We thus observe one of the dangers of narrative: at an extreme, one can indeed become nothing less than a prisoner of one's story. But there does remain hope in such cases. As the story of the second artist shows, reimagining and revivifying the past are integral to the process of keeping this hope alive. This person, too, found herself questioning her own viability as an artist. What she came to realize, in hindsight, is that she had become so thoroughly ensnared within the hermetic confines of art-world discourse that her own innermost interests and motives, and her own profound love of painting, had been utterly obscured. Only through identifying and naming the narrative she had unwittingly been living—which is to say, only by discerning the *truth*—could she break the stronghold of narrative foreclosure and thereby free herself to create once again.

Chapter 6, "The Truth of Story," seeks to work through this very idea. Drawing on an essay by Emily Fox Gordon entitled "Book of Days" (2003), I focus especially on the claim that autobiographies, memoirs, and other such memory-based life texts cannot help but falsify the past. Gordon, who had turned a personal essay into a full-blown memoir, bemoans the fact of having done so, not least because in her view the larger scope of the endeavor virtually ensured that she would succumb to the lure of fictionalizing the account. The result was a work that, despite its market value, had been irreparably tarnished—as in fact, Gordon suggests, all such works are doomed to be. Her claim is a disturbing one, and it is shared by many. I want to question this perspective, radically, and suggest that it derives from a too-limited view of reality and truth alike that is itself tied to a conception of time that is more appropriate to the world of *things* than to the world of *people*. In doing so, my primary aim in this chapter is to open up these three interrelated ideas in the hope of rescuing both hindsight and autobiographical narrative from their supposed doom.

The seventh and final chapter of the book, "The Good Life," seeks to bring together elements from the previous chapters, to present a more comprehensive picture of the role of hindsight in fashioning moral life. Drawing once more on Tolstoy's *The Death of Ivan Ilych* (1960 [1886]), I examine the connection between the backward movement of narrative and the forward movement of what, in psychological circles, goes by the name of "development," to show how the sort of moral clarification one is sometimes able to achieve through hindsight—most dramatically, perhaps, in the face of death—is itself a developmental achievement. Through narrative reflection there can be moral growth and "advance," such that the self is able, by degrees, to move forward to a better place. But as Tolstoy's story makes radiantly clear, the process is not only about the self; it is about the *Other*-than-self, that is, about those *goods*, outside the perimeter of the self, without which there can be neither development nor the deepening of moral life. The chapter is thus about how the work of hindsight is intimately tied to the work of being human, especially that part of it concerned with the question of how to live and what it might mean to live well.

I close the book with a coda, "Hindsight and Beyond," in which I give a fuller response to a question posed in Chapter 7: Given our condition of lateness—so painfully manifested in the story of Ivan Ilych—is there anything to be done about it? Strictly speaking, the answer is "No." The reason is that aspects of hindsight exist that are patently unsurpassable. For even if we had the capacity to see everything there was to be seen in any given moment, there still remains the fact that the meaning and significance of this moment will likely change as a function of what is to follow. Consequently, there will always be a "lag" between past and present, experience and hindsight; it is part and parcel of human temporality. I therefore go on to ask: What can be done to diminish this lag? In exploring this and a related question—how can we make ourselves morally better?—I identify various strategies for discerning the truth of our lives. The challenge, I suggest, is to live mindfully enough of the limits of one's perspective to allow more adequate perspectives into view. This can occur in the midst of ongoing experience. The task is to try as best one can to see experience for what it is when it is actually happening; that is, to be attentive enough to one's world, both outer and inner, to curb and correct then and there. It can also occur in reflection, through hindsight itself. As noted earlier, there is no questioning hindsight's capacity to distort and falsify; we can become trapped in our own stories and thereby prevent ourselves from seeing ourselves for what we truly are. But it is also through hindsight that we can pause, look again, and see ourselves anew, "unconcealed" by the urgencies of the moment. Looking backward, in hindsight, thus requires mindfulness in its own right. It is thus a vitally important means of interrogating our lives and, in so doing, learning and relearning, ever again, how to live.

ONE

HINDSIGHT, NARRATIVE, AND MORAL LIFE

LOOKING BACKWARD

"In hindsight," the newspaper story reads, "jumping in front of an oncoming subway train may not have been the smartest move Wesley Autrey has ever made. 'It's all hitting me now,'" he said. It was the day after Autrey had saved the life of a young man, apparently suffering from a medical problem, who had fallen onto the tracks as a train approached. Autrey knew he had to do something; if he didn't, the man would be dismembered. He therefore jumped from the platform down to the tracks and rolled with him into a drainage trough between the rails as the train hurtled into the station just a few inches above them. "Stupid" though Autrey had felt afterward, he certainly had no regrets. "I did something to save someone's life," he said. All's well that ends well.

But if all doesn't end well, what then? Here is another, rather more painful, story that took place back in 2003. It was the sixth game of the National League Championship Series in baseball, between the Chicago Cubs and the Florida Marlins. The Cubs hadn't won a World Series since 1908, and they hadn't even entered into one since 1945. But there they were, battling it out against the Marlins at Chicago's Wrigley Field, up three games to two in the series, and the score was 3–0 in the top of the eighth inning. The Marlins were up at bat, there was one out, two left to go. Victory was imminent, and the fans could taste it.

One of the Marlins banged out a double. And then, suddenly and inexplicably, everything came undone—"sheer disaster," as one sports writer put it. It all began with a fly ball down the left field line. The Cubs' left fielder, Moises Alou, raced toward the ball, which was heading foul. And just as Alou was about to make the catch, a fan—a Chicago Cubs fan, no less, Steve Bartman—reached out from the stands and deflected the ball. Oh well, one might say; someone prevented a foul ball from being caught. It was no big deal; he didn't even reach over the wall, so strictly speaking, it wasn't a case of fan interference. But that simple, dumb act, so innocent in its way—other fans had their arms outstretched too, and may well have done exactly the same thing had Steve Bartman not gotten there first—will echo through that poor man's life forever. Alou was enraged. The fans began booing and pelting Bartman with debris. And then, as if inevitably, more fuel was thrown on the fire. The Marlin player who had hit that fateful ball wound up walking. Two Marlins were now on base. A single followed, which drove in a run. Then there was an error on a ground ball. The bases are now loaded. There's another double, which knocks in two more runs: 3–3. A new pitcher comes in and intentionally walks the next batter, loading up the bases once more in the hope that, somehow, they'll be able to get an out, maybe two, and reel in the inning and the game. The crowd, meanwhile, sits in horrified silence. A sacrifice fly brings in another run, followed by yet another double, which brings in three more runs. One more run is knocked in by a single and, finally, mercifully, the Marlins are retired. The Cubs' at-bat during the bottom of that inning and the one to follow is utterly fruitless. The Marlins win, 8–3.

Forget about the walk, the hits, the error. The fingers point in one direction: *Bartman.* I prayed that the Cubs would win the seventh and final game of the series, if only to spare him a life that would likely be filled with grief and shame. If the Cubs were to win the final game, Bartman would simply have been a blip on the screen of history. He himself, of course, would never forget the incident, but he would probably be able to continue living in the Chicago area. If, on the other hand, the Cubs were to lose the final game, that day would become one of infamy, and he in turn would become one of the most loathed villains in that city's beleaguered history.

The next day was pitiful. Bartman (who had gone into hiding) had issued an apology in a prepared statement delivered by his brother-in-law that reads as follows: "I had my eyes glued on the approaching ball the entire time and was so caught up in the moment that I did not even see Moises Alou, much less that he may have had a play," he explained. "Had I thought for one second that the ball was playable or had I seen Alou approaching, I would have done whatever I could to get out of the way and give Alou a chance to make the catch." Bartman was a youth baseball coach, 26 years old. The night before, security guards had to escort him from Wrigley Field. After that, police had to keep watch over the suburban home he shared with his parents. "I am so truly sorry from the bottom of this Cubs fan's broken heart," the apology continued. "I ask that Cub fans everywhere redirect the negative energy that has been vented toward my family, my friends, and myself into the usual positive support for our beloved team on their way to becoming National Champs."

The Cubs lost again, 9–6, the following day, ending the series and their hopes for a World Series berth that year. Bartman

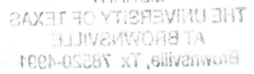

stayed home for this one, with the police. Thousands of people, including the governor of Illinois, blamed him for the role he had played in the Cubs' awful demise. Florida Governor Jeb Bush offered him asylum. He was also offered a free three-month stay at an ocean-front retreat in Pompano Beach.

Was Bartman really to be faulted for the Cubs' demise? Yes, apparently so. Sometimes the sheer force of history, pulsing along in its maddeningly saccadic way, is simply unbearable. There need to be causes, origins. Some fans would point to mysterious forces. There's a curse. It's bad karma. It's Destiny. Mythical thinking is at work here: there is the need to ward off the burden, even the *terror,* as the great historian of religion Mircea Eliade (1954) has put it, of fate, time, *history.* There is no room for accidents. Everything has a reason. Everything has a meaning. There is a story that can, and must, be told.

"In the phenomenalism of the 'inner world,'" Nietzsche (1968 [1888]) writes, "we invert the chronological order of cause and effect. The fundamental fact of 'inner experience' is that the cause is imagined after the effect has taken place" (p. 265). For Nietzsche, therefore, a kind of faulty reasoning is at work much of the time in human affairs, including baseball games. Historical time marches on in its irreversible, unpredictable way, and we humans, feeling the need to point fingers, insist on looking backward, imagining all the while that we're looking forward. It could be argued that we ought to be more dispassionately historical in how we think about these things. Bartman may have wished this himself. "This is how it unfolded," he might have said. "Don't forget about the error and the intentional walk, not to mention the entire seventh game. I'm not the only one to blame!" If only people could reconcile themselves to the facts of the matter. Why must memory be so fallible and so selective? Why must the whole of history—understood here as the unfolding of reality in all of its unpredictable messiness—be so alien to the human mind? Why does the end have to determine the beginning? Bartman's very life was in danger, one might argue, because most people just don't know how to think straight about What Really Happened. If only the Cubs had won that seventh game, everything would be entirely different. It would indeed; such is the nature of hindsight.

What we have been considering thus far is the hindsight that had been operative in the public response to Bartman's blunder. But what about Bartman's own response? One makes a decision—to reach for a foul ball—and the consequences jolt the future into a new form. In a case like his, the result is likely to be regret and shame, for one's blindness, one's inability to have seen what was going on. Remember what he had said in that pitiful plea: "Had I thought for one second that the ball was playable or had I seen Alou approaching, I would have done whatever I could to get out of the way and give Alou a chance to make the catch." Why, he might eventually ask, *didn't* I think for that one second? And how could I *not* have seen Alou approaching? He, of course, is trying to plead innocence here: *I didn't know.* Yes, he might continue, *now* I see what I have done. Should he really be blamed for getting caught up in the moment? It is one of humanity's defining features to do so. There can be the ecstasy of the felt abolition of time as we surrender ourselves to this or that spectacle, or act, or person— the power of *now.* But there can also be the horror of having become so thoroughly encased in the moment as to fail to recognize, to *see,* what exactly one is doing. There will be a delay, a postponement. Only later, after the moment has passed, will seeing be possible. *Oh, no.* Look at what I've done! *If only . . . .*

Let us briefly consider another story, this time from a work of fiction, that brings us still closer to the heart of the matter. In Leo Tolstoy's novella *The Death of Ivan Ilych* (1960 [1886]), we encounter a man who throughout much of his life had convinced himself that he had it all, that indeed everything was "as it should be" (p. 118). But then, after a seemingly minor household accident, things took a marked turn for the worse, both physically and psychically, ultimately leading Ivan Ilych to look back upon his life and to ask whether in fact it had been as good as he had assumed. Initially, this thought had been fleeting; given the decency and propriety of his life, given indeed that it seemed to be a veritable model of the good life, it was inconceivable that he could have made such a glaring mistake about who and what he had been. Eventually, however, he had to face the question more directly and honestly: Could it be that he had been wrong about his entire life? Could it be that he had actually *reversed* truth and falsity, and that the goodness that had seemed to characterize his life was not that at all but something superficial, even base? "It is as if I had been going downhill," Ilych says, "while I imagined I was going up" (p. 148). And all that remained was death. Was there anything to be done?

Tolstoy's extraordinary story, which I will address in greater detail in the final chapter of this book, is about many things: the tyranny of bourgeois niceties, the terrible weak spots of the human heart, the primacy and elision of death. But it is also about the limits of our capacity to see what's going on when it's going on and in turn about the potential power of hindsight to reveal—and I say this cautiously—the true nature of things. This is a radical move on Tolstoy's part. Oftentimes, what is happening now, in the moment, is seen as Reality and hindsight as a source of distortion and error: Compared to the fleshy immediacy of the present, so manifestly *there* before us, the backward gaze of memory, with its desires and designs, and its distance from the past-present of experience, can seem like a gauzy veil, if not an outright source of bald-faced lies, unconsciously crafted to reassure ourselves that our lives are meaningful, coherent, good.

All this is potentially true of hindsight, and psychologists, among many others, have been quick to point it out. In an article entitled "Hindsight: Biased judgments of past events after the outcomes are known" (1990), for instance, Scott Hawkins and Reid Hastie speak of the projection of outcome knowledge onto the past accompanied by a denial that this knowledge has influenced judgment. They thus speak of "hindsight bias," which is "the tendency for people with outcome knowledge to believe falsely that they would have predicted the reported outcome of an event" (p. 311). They would have "known it all along," or so they say. "Once people know the outcome of an event," Ralph Hertwig, Carola Fanselow, and Ulrich Hoffrage (2003) add, "they tend to overestimate what could have been anticipated in foresight" (p. 357).[1] Hindsight bias, the argument generally continues, is but an example of the much more general phenomenon of memory distortion.[2] There is talk in this body of work not only of "retrospective bias," which according to Daniel Schacter and Elaine Scarry (2000) reveals that "one's memories of past experiences can be influenced by one's current beliefs" (p. 3), but also of memory's many "sins" (Schacter, 2001), which range from transience ("a weakening or loss of memory over time" [p. 4]) to misattribution ("assigning memory to the

---

[1] See also Fischoff, 1975; Hoffrage and Pohl, 2003.
[2] See especially Schacter's, 1995, edited volume; see also Schacter, 1996, 2001; Schacter and Scarry, 2000.

wrong source" [p. 5]) to the infamous suggestibility ("which refers to memories that are implanted as a result of leading questions, comments, or suggestions when a person is trying to call up a past experience" [p. 5]). Other problems exist as well, more directly related to hindsight as it functions in autobiographical reflection. It can be defensive; it can create an illusory appearance of order and coherence; it can interweave the real and the imagined in a way that utterly falsifies the past. And, as we shall see in Chapter 6, when it assumes the form of an actual autobiographical text, the problems at hand may be magnified. None of what I have to say here, therefore, should be taken to imply that hindsight is problem-free. But the predominant emphasis on bias, distortion, and falsification has largely occluded the more positive potential at hand.

This suggests that we need to think about hindsight in a quite different way—one that allows for the possibility not only of distortion but insight, not only of lies but truth. Indeed, some truths can *only* be attained in hindsight, via what I am here calling *narrative reflection*. For all the power that "now" may have, it is also saddled with definite limits. In his classic essay on the "Conditions and limits of autobiography" (1980), Georges Gusdorf puts the matter as follows:

> An examination of consciousness limited to the present moment will give me only a fragmentary cutting from my personal being without guarantee that it will continue. . . . In the immediate moment, the agitation of things ordinarily surrounds me too much for me to be able to see it in its entirety. Memory gives me a certain remove and allows me to take into consideration all the ins and outs of the matter, its context in time and space. As an aerial view sometimes reveals to an archeologist the direction of a road or a fortification or the map of a city invisible to someone

on the ground, so the reconstruction in spirit of my destiny bares the major lines that I have failed to notice, the demands of the deepest values I hold that, without my being clearly aware of it, have determined my most decisive choices. (p. 38)

So it is that we must often await the future in order to discern more fully the meaning and significance of what has gone on in the past.

But the limits at hand are not only temporal, a function of the "agitation of things," the flux and indeterminacy that frequently characterize immediate experience. They are also a function of *one's own* limits—one's shortsightedness, as I referred to it earlier. This is particularly so in the moral domain, where we tend to act first and think later. Along these lines, one might say that there frequently exists a kind of "autism" to the now, an egoistic—and at times egocentric—absence of perspective. Through hindsight, through the distance of self from self conferred through hindsight, this autism can be surmounted. Hindsight, in assuming the form of narrative reflection, thus emerges as a potential vehicle not only of *truth* but *goodness* and should therefore be understood as a key player in strengthening and deepening moral life.

AFTER THE FACT

In my previous book on these issues, *Rewriting the Self: History, Memory, Narrative* (1993), my concerns were largely methodological. Against the backdrop of what I perceived to be the sterility of a good deal of contemporary psychological inquiry, I saw in life narratives an antidote, a vehicle for introducing a much-needed measure of humanity into the discipline. My aim was to study lives, the stories of lives, and my question was how to do so in a way that was responsible, valuable, and legitimate. In large measure, *Rewriting the Self* was about the requisite conditions for generating narrative understanding and knowledge. As such, I needed to explore such issues as the reliability of memory, the relationship between language and personal identity, the nature of life historical "facts," the problem of interpretation, and, finally, the value of narrative methodology for exploring the human realm.

Many of these issues remain relevant to the present undertaking. But here, my focus has shifted. Narrative, I want to argue, is not only to be considered a privileged vehicle for exploring the human realm, it is a primary inroad into understanding human life and human selfhood. Right away, however, problems emerge. Life is not itself narrative, many have argued. By drawing the two too closely together, the argument may continue, one runs the risk of rendering life in too orderly a fashion and thereby flattening out its vagaries, its palpable lack, at times, of coherence, meaning, story-like followability. My initial response to such arguments was to challenge them by positing what I held to be the continuity between living and telling. By and large, I still tend to gravitate to this point of view, for reasons that will become clear soon enough.

In recent years, however, I have found myself more willing, and perhaps able, to see the other side. Quite honestly, the reason has little to do with the cogency of the arguments presented. Indeed, I continue to find that many of those who argue for the *dis*continuity between living and telling have a somewhat impoverished view of both: living is likely to be portrayed as formless flux, while narrative is likely to be portrayed in terms of those well-crafted stories with readily discerned beginnings, middles, and ends. And consequently (the argument goes), it follows that the latter must have precious little to do with the former. This view is wrongheaded. And yet, there does remain a notable gap between what we humans can know of immediate experience, in the moment, and what we can see, sometimes joyfully, sometimes painfully, in retrospect. As I have argued in some recent work, in fact, human existence may be characterized as involving a *delay*, or "postponement," of insight into its affairs.[3] Realizations, narrative connections, are made after-the-fact, when the dust has settled. The result, as Tolstoy's story shows with radiant and tragic clarity, is that we are frequently *late* in our own understanding of things. Hindsight, in turn, may be said to perform a kind of "rescue" function: by taking up what could not, or would not, be seen in the immediacy of the moment, it can rescue us from the oblivion that so often characterizes the human condition. It thus emerges as a fundamental tool for ethical and moral *recollection,* taken here in the classical sense of "gathering together" that which would otherwise be lost owing to our pervasive tendency toward forgetfulness.

I do not mean to suggest that hindsight is pain-free or that it is always redemptive. On the one hand, it can be a vehicle of insight and, at times, a source of deep fulfillment: I can realize what is truly important or, for that matter, unimportant about this or that feature of my past experience; I can see the contours of people I care for more clearly; I can look back on an event, or a period of life that had seemed commonplace, ordinary, and find in its very ordinariness a source of pleasure and gratitude for it having existed at all. On the other hand, hindsight can be a source of regret and remorse, guilt and shame: I look back on my past and can find my own shortsightedness or wastefulness

---

[3] See especially Freeman, 2003a.

or cowardice (pick your sin) downright staggering. Here, too, there can be insight, but of the sort that hurts. Hindsight is thus an arena of both promise and peril, pleasure and pain.

This pain can itself be of immense value for the project not only of ethical and moral recollection, but also of self-transcendence and personal development. For, even in the course of identifying my own culpability, I have begun to move to a better place, a place where I have the chance to see my past anew and to evolve a new vision of myself and of my role in the world. Pain may of course remain in such a situation. I may, for instance, be so staggered by my culpability that, despite my insight, despite my perch from this better place, I am paralyzed, unable to find any redeeming value in what I have learned. We shall hear more about this sort of situation later on, when we explore some of the work of Primo Levi. There can also be the pain entailed in the felt impossibility of *undoing* the past, which can culminate in what I have called "narrative foreclosure," the conviction that one's story is effectively over. In cases such as these, some measure of reconciliation will be needed, some attempt to resign oneself both to the permanence of the past's events and to one's own finitude and fallibility. But even in these cases, there remains room for growth. If Tolstoy is right, there even remains the possibility for (some measure of) redemption: as gruesome and horrific as Ivan Ilych's last days were, he did manage to gain some much-needed solace before he succumbed. Late though we may be, therefore, it may still be possible to find a better way. But the process can be arduous, indeed.

THE BIRTH OF HINDSIGHT

How did this process come to be, and how did it acquire the significance it has? Because the process of looking backward over the terrain of the personal past is so much a part of the modern experience, we may think of it as natural, a fundamental dimension of human memory and self-exploration. By all accounts, however, the kind of recollective self-reckoning that we have been considering was a long time coming, requiring an attitude and relationship to the personal past that emerged as part of a much larger socio-historical constellation having to do with the very nature of personhood. In his book *The Myth of the Eternal Return* (1954), Mircea Eliade considers both the phenomenology of time consciousness in "archaic" societies and the massive divide that separates these societies from ones such as our own. "In studying these traditional societies, one characteristic has especially struck us," he writes: "it is their revolt against concrete, historical time, their nostalgia for a periodical return to the mythical time of the beginning of things, to the 'Great Time'" (p. ix). His subject matter is therefore "archaic ontology," as he puts it—"more precisely, the conceptions of being and reality that can be read from the behavior of the man of the premodern societies" (p. 3), including both the world referred to as "primitive" and the ancient cultures of Asia, Europe, and America. As Eliade goes on to explain,

> In the particulars of his conscious behavior, the "primitive," the archaic man, acknowledges no act which has not previously been posited and lived by someone else, some other being who was not a man. What he does has been done before. His life is the ceaseless repetition of gestures initiated by others. This conscious repetition of given paradigmatic gestures reveals an original ontology. The crude product of nature, the object fashioned by the industry of man, acquire their reality, their identity, only to the extent of their participation in a

transcendent reality. The gesture acquires meaning, reality, solely to the extent to which it repeats a primordial act. (p. 5)

In the context of ritual especially, "concrete time," located in the sensuous present, "is projected into mythical time, *in illo tempore*"—in those days—"when the foundation of the world occurred," the ritual having been "performed for the first time by a god, an ancestor, or a hero" (pp. 20–21).[4]

It is important to emphasize that, according to Eliade, historical time—conceived broadly in terms of linearity and irreversibility—was unquestionably a part of the archaic world. It's not as if archaic peoples had no idea at all about history; it's that they found it deeply problematic and alien to their innermost concerns. Historical time was, fundamentally, empty time, devoid of meaning precisely because of its accidental, ephemeral quality. "An object or act becomes real" for these people "only insofar as it repeats an archetype. Thus, reality is acquired solely through repetition or participation; everything which lacks an exemplary model is 'meaningless,' i.e., it lacks reality" (p. 34). In sum: "any meaningful act performed by archaic man, any real act, i.e., any repetition of an archetypal gesture, suspends duration, abolishes profane time, and participates in mythical time" (p. 36).

Also significant is the view of personhood that accompanies the mythical worldview. Here, I turn once more to Georges Gusdorf (1980). "Throughout most of human history," he writes, "the individual does not oppose himself to all others; he does not feel himself to exist outside of others, and still less against others, but very much *with* others in an interdependent existence that asserts its rhythms everywhere in the community"

---

[4] See also Freeman, 1998; Kearney, 2001.

(p. 28). As a consequence of this thoroughgoing interdependence, Gusdorf continues,

> No one is rightful possessor of his life or his death; lives are so thoroughly entangled that each of them has its center everywhere and its circumference nowhere. The important unit is thus never the isolated being—or, rather, isolation is impossible in such a scheme of total cohesiveness as this. Community life unfolds like a great drama, with its climactic moments originally fixed by the gods being repeated from age to age. Each man thus appears as the possessor of a role, already performed by the ancestors and to be performed again by descendants, [with the result that] the community maintains a continuous self-identity in spite of the constant renewal of individuals who constitute it. (pp. 28–29)

In line with Eliade's ideas, Gusdorf goes on to discuss the correlation between mythic structures and the principle of repetition: "Theories of eternal recurrence, accepted in various guises as dogma by the majority of the great cultures of antiquity, fix attention on that which remains, not on that which passes. 'That which is,' according to the wisdom of Ecclesiastes, 'is that which has been, and there is nothing new under the sun'" (p. 29).

We can therefore see why mythical time brings alongside it what might be termed a "sociocentric" conception of personhood: insofar as one views his or her life through the prism of recurrent mythical forms, personhood becomes indissociable from the eternally present nexus of social relations.[5] Even

---

[5] Shweder & Bourne, 1984.

in ancient Greece, generally considered the fundamental wellspring of Western culture, the notion of the individual, and individuated, person was not to be found. Nor was the genre of autobiography. Rather than fashioning narratives that were personal and private, the primary concern of the person was to become integrated into the community; thinking about one's existence, therefore, was inseparable from thinking about the communal world.[6] The Greek sense of self was thus deeply embedded in a cultural whole. Only later would there emerge the possibility of this self "standing out" from its broader social context of being. And only later would it become appropriate for a person to seize upon his or her personal memories, or "life stories," and relate them to others in the form of autobiography. This process would be nothing short of a "cultural revolution," wherein humanity "emerged from the mythic framework of traditional teachings and ... entered into the perilous domain of history" (Gusdorf, 1980, p. 30).

The emergence of the "autobiographical subject," as we might call it, is thus inseparable from the emergence of historical consciousness and the privileging of historical time:

The man who takes the trouble to tell of himself knows that the present differs from the past and that it will not be repeated in the future; he has become more aware of differences than of similarities; given the constant change, given the uncertainty of events and of men, he believes it a useful and valuable thing to fix his own image so that he can be certain it

---

[6] See Freeman & Brockmeier, 2001; also Vernant, 1995.

> will not disappear like all things in this world. (Gusdorf, 1980,
> p. 30)

In place of eternal recurrence and essential sameness there is
change and difference; in place of certainty, uncertainty and
accident; in place of perpetual reappearance, disappearance and
death, the sense of an ending, final and irrevocable. The emergence of historical consciousness and historical time therefore
brings in tow a quite different conception of personhood than
the sociocentric one identified earlier with the mythical worldview. There is now the "individualization" of persons, the ever-
present threat of death, and, more generally, the replacement of
the archetypal pattern, embodied in the circle, with the historical
trajectory, embodied in the line. There is also the emergence of
hindsight "proper," such that one gazes back over the terrain of
the personal past, seeking to discern new meanings, ones that had
been unavailable in the flux of the immediate. Meaning thus
becomes "unhinged" and mobile, as much a function of "now" as
"then." A dimension of difference, of *deferral,* has emerged such
that, henceforth, the project of *knowing,* particularly *self-*
knowing, becomes inextricably bound to looking backward.

It also becomes bound to the idea of moral *accountability.*[7] It
might be noted in this context that accounting for one's actions
in court was one of the few occasions in Greek culture in which
an individual might have told a first-person narrative.[8] This
should serve to remind us that such accounts were in fact
possible far earlier than is sometimes assumed. By all indications, however, it is not until the fourth century C.E., when

---

[7] Freeman & Brockmeier, 2001.
[8] See Most, 1989.

St. Augustine wrote his *Confessions* (1980; originally 397) that we find accountability assuming the form of narrative reflection. So it is that philosopher Charles Taylor, in *Sources of the Self* (1989), writes of the "radical reflexivity" that bursts upon the scene with the *Confessions* and "brings to the fore a kind of presence to oneself which is inseparable from one's being the agent of experience," that is, one "with a first-person standpoint" (p. 131). Indeed, it is Augustine's great work that is generally taken to represent the inauguration of that sort of looking-back process that may be linked to the reflective work of hindsight and in turn to the genre of autobiography.

There are other significant players in this story. Descartes is surely one, as are Montaigne, Rousseau, and Goethe, each of whom inaugurate new, and still more internalized, dimensions of narrative reflection. For present purposes, however, it is Augustine who remains the key player. Taylor's thesis regarding the emergence of radical reflexivity gives us some helpful clues for why this is so. Historian Karl Weintraub, in *The Value of the Individual: Self and Circumstance in Autobiography* (1978), fills in some vitally important details. As Weintraub notes, others before Augustine had written of great deeds or of memorable events they had witnessed. There had also been stories of how certain individuals had become "wise men," philosophers. "(B)ut none opened up their souls in the inwardness of genuine autobiography" (p. 1), seeing in their stories a means of coming to terms with their very existence. This is not the only reason, however, for the *Confessions* being as revolutionary as it was. As Weintraub also notes, Augustine's entire appraisal of his life is filtered through the conversion experience he had eventually undergone. The *Confessions* thus belongs to "that type of autobiography in which one datable moment in life enables a human being to order all his experience retrospectively by the insight of one momentous turn" (p. 25). In virtually any autobiographical endeavor, a process exists whereby experience is ordered retrospectively. With Augustine, however, a full-scale shift of meaning is brought about by his newfound circumstances. Weintraub refers to the centrality of "presentness," such that the act of confession becomes identified with "self-searching, self-questioning, self-discovery, self-description, and self-assessment" (p. 26). What we thus see, in a quite unprecedented way, is the centrality of hindsight and narrative in undertaking this restless probing of the self. "My life" becomes a paramount concern; living, in turn, is supplemented by telling, the result being "my story," worthy in its own right but in some instances worthy enough for others to learn about as well. In this story, there will almost surely be painful moments of decision but also twists and turns, accidents and unanticipated consequences, and, not least, considerations of the difference between life as it had been lived, in all of its uncertainty and unknowingness, and life as it appears now, through the eyes of the present. In a distinct sense, the phenomenon of hindsight presupposes this very difference.

As both Taylor and Weintraub go on to note, an important distinction should be made between Augustine's autobiographical search and those forms of narrative reflection that emerge as we move closer to modernity. Radically inward though his search is, it remains driven and directed by God. As Taylor (1989) puts the matter, "God," in Augustine's story, "is not just what we long to see, but what powers the eye which sees. So the light of God is not just 'out there,' illuminating the order of being, ... ; it is also an 'inner' light" (p. 129). For Weintraub (1978), the Augustinian project may even be seen as a "premature" version of the search for self, owing to its very dependence on God. While it unquestionably represents "a historicizing of human realities which the classical mentality

... could not have achieved, it is still only a step toward that historicist view of the self-concept on which the notion of individuality depends" (p. 47). Only a step: Augustine's mode of self-reflection and self-understanding, operating via a new-found and indeed revolutionary reliance on hindsight, is not yet "there"—i.e., *here*. According to Weintraub, it remains pre-historicist, pre-individual, pre-*us*.

For Augustine, in any case, the path inward was, in the end, the path upward. In modern times, it is often suggested, this upward path was largely superseded by a more thoroughgoing process of interiorization, a movement toward the inner land-scape of the self. For better or for worse, the story generally continues, we are left with ourselves, our only hope being that the depths we are thought to possess will suffice to bring us some measure of meaning. While Taylor's story is a somewhat tragic one, entailing a lamentable loss of divine direction, and Weintraub's is a more "presenticentric" tale of progress, they nevertheless agree that something momentous followed the Augustinian revolution: God, or Good, the supposition of a transcendent order giving form and meaning to personal exis-tence, progressively fades from the picture, leaving individuals to their own, largely inner devices. Hindsight, in turn, becomes a matter of wrestling with one's inner demons, of discerning how one has fared in relation to one's own innermost standards and ideals. Pride, gratitude, and what Erik Erikson (e.g., 1994) refers to as "integrity" may emerge when, upon looking back-ward over the landscape of my life, I see what I have done and been, what I have made of my own unique world. Conversely, I may feel shame, resentment, disappointment, and despair upon viewing my life's wreckage: to think that I have fallen so sorely short of what I could be.

But here we might ask: To what extent have we completely abandoned a reliance on transcendent sources? What does it mean to say that I am "grateful" for my life or that I am "disappointed" in it, that I have realized, or not realized, my own unique potential or calling? These are statements that unquestionably refer to an inner landscape. It is also of course true that, for many, there is no God supporting the process; the ardent atheist can surely wrestle with his or her own demons without invoking anyone or anything larger than the self so embroiled. Even in this instance, though, does there not remain a transcendent horizon, the felt conviction that there is *some* order, or principle, or value that exists beyond me and that conditions the self-judgments and self-appraisals I make? As shall be clear in the pages to follow, Augustine's legacy is very much with us still, not only in the radical reflexivity and retrospective reordering that characterize narrative reflection but in the inseparability of such reflection from fundamental questions concerning the nature, purpose, and meaning of life itself.

TWO

THE NARRATIVE IMAGINATION

THE BEGINNING OF THE END

Recall for a moment the Steve Bartman debacle recounted in Chapter 1. Even though numerous other events had culminated in the Cubs' demise, fingers had been pointed at him, as if he had been the cause of it all. Were Bartman to try to defend himself, I suggested, he might have enlisted the help of those students of memory who emphasize the pernicious operation of hindsight bias, our pervasive tendency to falsify the past by seeing it through present eyes. There are, however, at least two additional accounts that might be given. First, there is the simple "he ought to have known" account. On this account, what Bartman did was just plain stupid and, our inclination to get "caught up in the moment" notwithstanding, he deserved all the grief he received. But there is another way of framing these issues as well. Whether he did so intentionally or not, Bartman inaugurated a *narrative*—a narrative of a quite different order than the one that appeared to be in the making during that fateful game. Hence the shock and disbelief that befell so many people watching the game: in a matter of moments, comedy had been transformed into tragedy. And all of the lamentations of "if only" had come hurtling forward, leaving the afflicted with the awful sense that time was running out and there wasn't a blessed thing to do about it. It was too late, the beginning of the end.

After another tragic baseball game in which the Red Sox lost to the Yankees (in the American League Championship Series that same year), a friend of mine told me that, in a way, the loss had been good for his teenage son. I don't recall his exact words, but he said something that suggested that the boy had never experienced real loss before. Real loss?! We can hear the refrain: *It's only a game.* But there can be real loss in a lost game. This is because the forces set in motion in the contained arena of the sports event entail a radical compression of some of the most basic temporal rhythms we know. There is, for example, the beautiful redemptive momentum of the dream about to be fulfilled. In the seventh inning of the Red Sox game, with the Sox ahead 5–2, I looked over to my wife and giddily proclaimed that they might actually pull this one off. There was land in sight, a safe harbor. We were heading there, finally. Unbelievable!

Then, there may be a phase of existential vertigo, where everything is wide open and uncertain: something is happening, but it's not clear what. In true existential fashion, there can be real anxiety at this point. Hope and dread become fused together into a kind of high-pitched inner scream. You're nowhere. You want to look and can't bear to look. There may be salvation. There may be perdition. It's at this juncture that one will often hear people mutter, "I can't take this."

As for the next phase, there is the brutal, chaotic fall, made that much more acute by the fact that, just minutes ago, it had seemed that triumph was actually in sight. The giddier the expectation, the sharper the descent of the fall and the more it becomes suffused with despairing shock. This is no garden-variety disappointment. This is *suffering*. And minor-league though it may be in the general scheme of things, the essential *form* of the suffering is actually much the same as it is in more dire situations. What's more, the aforementioned feature of compression, the fact that everything is happening so quickly, within the enclosure of a game, intensifies the essential features of the form. Set against the *truly* catastrophic, the content of the sporting event is trivial. But given the resonance of the sports-induced emotional experience with other, more horrific experiences and given as well the temporal compression involved, it seems perfectly justified to speak of there having been a sense of real loss for many.

One is reminded here of Aristotle's discussion of the "structuring of the incidents" in tragedy, which is described as "an imitation not of men but of a life." By structuring of the incidents, Aristotle is speaking of *plot*, which he describes as "the basic principle, the heart and soul, as it were, of tragedy" (1973, p. 28). This brings us closer to the core of the issue. The kinds of temporal rhythms set in motion by the structure of the events that took place that year, on those beautiful baseball diamonds, need a home in the human mind. Narrative is the home for these rhythms; it's what we have available to make sense of our existence in time.

I have sympathy for Bartman. In a distinct sense, he had become the victim of our own drive toward narrative, toward finding meaning in a life that sometimes seems utterly inexplicable. The "objective" historian or the empiricist memory researcher, on the lookout for distortion, might wish to exonerate him. He or she might dig up a film of Bartman, straining for that ball with lots of other like-minded fans. There would be talk of the error that followed, the hits, the runs, the next game—all of the different, very real factors that culminated in the Cubs' demise. This might be framed as the True Account of What Really Happened. It might have some value too. Maybe it would jar some people into recognizing that causation in history is a plural matter, that a given outcome is often "overdetermined," the terminus of numerous contributory streams.

But this rendition of What Really Happened, whatever its claims to objectivity may be, would likely remain unsatisfactory to many. In part, this is because we tend to be historical simplifiers, even reducers, who often skate over the relevant facts in order to lay the blame *somewhere* rather than everywhere or nowhere. In a related vein, this sort of account might also prove unsatisfactory because of the terror of history, because of our deep-seated reluctance to embrace the accidental and irrevocable nature of things. Finally, though, it would be unsatisfactory because of our drive toward narrative, our "narrative intelligence," as philosopher Paul Ricoeur (1991) calls it, which insists on seeing-together a sequence of events and situating them within those broad categories of plot—in this case, tragedy—that allow us to derive some measure of order and meaning in a sometimes frightful world.

Grady Little, the Red Sox manager whose decision to retain a then-flagging pitcher (Pedro Martinez) on the mound cost his team that game with the Yankees, had complained about this situation. It was a matter of narrative *un*intelligence, he might have said. "A lot of people have the answers," he said, "after the results come in." Little was not about to cry over any spilled milk. If given the chance, he, unlike poor Bartman, would do the very same thing all over again. (Or so he said.) Nietzsche (1974 [1887]) enters the scene once more with his image of the eternal return: give me the opportunity to return to that fateful game, along with everything that came before, and I'd seize it with pleasure. The decision Little had made was hardly something to celebrate. But he would have no problem sleeping at night. He was no Ivan Ilych, whose infernal screaming, for three days running, "was so terrible that one could not hear it through two closed doors without horror" (Tolstoy, 1960 [1886], p. 154). What's done is done! "I know that wherever I go, I'll do the best I can," Little had said. "I know what we did there," he avows. "I'm sorry the results of one decision caused so much pain, and it sure helped sell a lot of papers. But gol'dang, I can't turn back the clock and make another decision, not knowing whether the results of that decision are good or not."

Little is surely right to remind us that "You can't turn back the clock." He is also right to point toward our pervasive tendency to let endings determine beginnings. This is simply not how clocks work; the arrow of time points forward, not backward. But we live in the time not only of clocks, in which events come along, one after the other, but also of narrative, in which the storyline is of the essence. Whether Bartman or Little like it or not, the outcome—the ending—*matters*. It's not a detachable conclusion but is instead the final episode of an emerging pattern, an evolving story, integrally related to what has come before. I am not suggesting for a moment that Bartman and Little ought to have been tarred and feathered; there remains ample room for humanity in the perspective being offered here. What I am suggesting is that it makes perfect sense that, as Little had put it, "A lot of people have the answers after the results come in." It also makes sense that, in view of the results, some contributions are singled out more than others. Such is the nature of hindsight.

An important question remains. Is the hypothetical account given before, of What Really Happened, the true one? Does singling out Bartman and Little entail a falsification of the past, derived perhaps from that lingering mythopoeic impulse I spoke of earlier, a vestigial desire to people the world with gods and demons, heroes and villains? Is hindsight, finally, testimony to the feebleness of the human mind, its pervasive tendency to distort reality? My answer to these questions is an emphatic "No." This is because the question of What Really Happened is not a matter of facts alone. Indeed, I would go so far as to say that ordinarily we do not, and cannot, know What Really Happened until there is an ending. This is the way of narrative, and it is every bit as real as the events that happen along, clock ticking all the while.

POEISIS

Thus far, I have tried to suggest that hindsight, while certainly a potential source of bias and distortion, can also serve as a vehicle for gaining insight into the personal past—especially into those features of the personal past that one either could not or would not see in the immediacy of the present moment. So it is that hindsight, far from necessarily occluding the truth, may at times be the requisite condition for attaining it. In a related vein, I also suggested that hindsight is a prime vehicle for rescuing moral life. One of the tragic truths of the human condition is that we are often morally "late": caught up in this or that moment, with its limited view of things, it is often only later, with the passage of time, that we can see the errors of our ways. From one vantage point, this process may be seen as little more than an attempt to shore up our present selves by derogating our past selves.[1] From another vantage point, however, it may be seen as a vitally

---

[1] See Ross, 1991; Ross & Wilson, 2000.

important corrective to the moral shortsightedness that so often characterizes our experience in the moment.

Both of these dimensions of hindsight are themselves the products of *poiesis,* which in broad outline refers to that sort of constructive, imaginative activity that is involved in our various efforts to make sense of the world, both outer and inner. To "make sense of": in this simple term, there is reference both to "making," in the sense of a kind of constructive doing, and to "explicating," in the sense of discerning what is actually there, in the world. As I have suggested elsewhere (see Freeman, 1993), poets strive neither for a mimetic representation of the world nor for a fictive imposition upon it. Rather, they seek to *rewrite* the world through the imagination, such that we, readers, can see or feel something about it that might otherwise have gone unnoticed or undisclosed. As the poet and essayist Yves Bonnefoy (1989) has noted, "this world which cuts itself off from the world seems to the person who creates it not only more satisfying than the first but also more real" (p. 164). Bonnefoy goes on to speak of the "impression of a reality at last fully incarnate, which comes to us, paradoxically, through words which have turned away from incarnation" (p. 164). Poetry, poetic language, rather than entailing the imposition of meaning, entails *disclosure,* "unconcealedness," as Heidegger (1971) calls it, its aim being nothing less than the revelation of truth. Along these lines, poetry seeks to depict the "realer than real"; it is an effort to move beyond the exterior of things and thereby to actualize the potential of meaning the world bears within it. Notice here the parallel between hindsight and poetry: just as hindsight may disclose meanings that might have been unavailable in the immediacy of the moment, poetry may disclose meanings, and truths, that might otherwise have gone unarticulated. Both are thus potential vehicles of what might be termed *recuperative disclosure;* they are agents of insight and rescue, recollection and recovery, serving to counteract the forces of oblivion.

Let us now move beyond this parallel and explore in greater detail the poetic moment of hindsight itself. I do so with some trepidation: the hindsight in question is my own, and I have no interest whatsoever in "unconcealing" too much about my*self.* My aim is instead to "use" myself, as it were, in order to talk about something else—in this case, the nature of the narrative imagination. To begin, I turn to an event that, while simple and routine in its way at the time, has turned out to be among the most memorable of my entire life.

MYTH AND MONUMENT

My father could scarcely have imagined that I would someday be writing book chapters such as this one. In fact, there was a sizable span of time during which the distinct possibility must have been raised in my family that, whatever I would do in life, it would be precious little. I don't want to create the wrong impression here. It's not as if I was condemned or considered a blot on the family name or some such thing; I was loved, cared for, played with, and all the rest. But my dad died very suddenly when I was quite young; I had just turned 20. And at that particular time, given the kind of life I seemed most interested in living, it simply wasn't clear yet how everything would turn out.

Part of the problem was my age. I have two older brothers, one eight years older and one six. By the time I graduated from high school, they were each married, were beginning to build their own families, and, in general, were well on their way to becoming "established." The oldest one had graduated from Georgetown and NYU Law and, despite having been something of a radical in college, which occasionally made for some rather heated exchanges with my father at the dinner table, had eventually gotten it together. And when he and his wife produced a beautiful baby girl early in July of 1975, in the bloom of summer, all of that tension seemed to melt away. As for my other brother, who had been valedictorian of his high school class, who had graduated something-or-other *cum laude* from Yale, who had gotten married to a Wonderful Girl from a Good Family at age 21, who had gone on to Harvard Business School, only to land shortly thereafter at Procter and Gamble, where he would market diapers for the nation's young and helpless, the only thing he was missing was a Purple Heart or a Presidential Medal of Honor. He was a dutiful son too. Not too long after I was appointed an assistant professor, he told me that he would have sooner thought I would be in jail than in a classroom. He said it with a smile, but on some level he meant it. Not only was I the baby of the family, who had been spoiled, "got away with murder," and so on, but in his eyes at least I had been something of a wild man, who had already done some things that he himself would never have *dreamed* of doing, particularly given the much-mythicized wrath of my father.

The myth goes something like this: My two brothers, living under my dad's reign of terror, had been forced to walk the straight and narrow path; when they were my age, there had been no room for shenanigans, back-talk, broken curfews, or anything else that gave the slightest hints of disobedience or disrespect. By the time I came along, my dad had mellowed a bit, the times were a-changing, and, by my brothers' account, my life had been one great big fun-fest, in which I had been able to do everything they had not. In any case, set in contrast to the clean-shaven family men my brothers had become, there is no doubt but that I must have seemed like a different kind of creature altogether. There is a picture of my father and me—I was around 18 at the time—in which we're standing outside on a sunny winter day. He's in a woolen coat, strong and serious, with a thick mustache, gazing sternly at the camera. I'm standing apart from him, in a two-tone suede jacket, hair halfway down my chest, with just the tiniest smirk on my face. In some ways, we were worlds apart.

I fear I might be giving the wrong impression again. It is true that my dad had a temper. He never, ever laid a hand on any of us, but the way he would sometimes yell at us, like he was ready to boil over with rage, would actually lead us to wish he would just whack us and get it over with. I can also remember a number of incidents (one, for instance, involving his response to the poor fellow who made the mistake of giving him the finger during the course of some jockeying in traffic) when he was downright scary. So there is no denying that he could be a pretty tough character. But he was also funny and charming, passionately in love with my mother, warm and affectionate with his children, playful with the family dog, greatly enamored of food and drink and nice clothes and traveling and dancing and many other things besides. For all of his rage and occasional sullenness, he was immensely entertaining, a larger-than-life figure with a great sense of humor. He loved to imitate new-borns' faces. Proud parents would ooh and aah over their new babies, gushing over how cute they were or how much they look liked so-and-so; and as soon as we were out the door, he would be making a dopey baby-face, poking fun at how sappy and deluded people were about their wondrous offspring. "For Chrissake, they all look the same!" And he kissed me, or I kissed him, each and every night before bed, for as long as our lives intersected. There was tenderness and the smell of shaving lotion and a sense of real—albeit unspoken—connection. It was so long ago: 35 years now. Why did it have to be? *Why?* The death of a parent can leave wounds that never fully heal.

For a while, during my youth, everything no doubt seemed kind of touch-and-go to my parents. When I was in tenth grade, an able but not exactly driven student, I became a member of a "gang" of sorts—not a chain-wielding, black-leather-jacket gang of the sort that "hoods" or "tree-boys" (tough New York boys, with greasy hair, who counted "one, two, tree") formed, but a good-time gang, a bunch of guys who became bonded together in friendship and, every now and then, mayhem. We called ourselves the "Misty Mountain Maulers," Misty Mountain having been taken from the pages of Tolkien's *The Hobbit.* We had special shirts made up (I still have mine) and commenced what we called a "Viking Feast," a bacchanalian food-and-drink fest which, as it turns out, we have held every year but two since 1971. It was, and still is, great fun.

We were a ragged bunch, to say the least. We had contests to see who could grow their hair the longest and in turn annoy our parents the most. My good friend Lew, whose hair eventually reached his waist, when it was wet at least, was the winner. I wasn't far behind. We also loved basketball, a few of us played lacrosse, and we communicated mainly through sarcastic jokes and what we then thought were intellectually penetrating commentaries on the absurdities of the New York suburban life we were all leading. Everything we did was filled with irony; despite our profound closeness, it was the only way we knew how to talk with one another. I also shouldn't neglect to mention the fact that we were bonded by books as well, especially roguish adventure stories like Kerouac's *On the Road* and heavy existentialist novels by Sartre and Camus and Kafka. We fancied ourselves as being living contradictions; we were madcap literary jock good old boys, shuttling between parties and poetry.

There were a few serious crises. I, for instance, was almost killed in a car accident the summer after eleventh grade—intensive care unit, critical condition, lots of broken bones, the whole bit. My dad passed out cold the moment he saw me. I wouldn't wish it upon anyone, but some good actually came of it. For one, some of the incessant squabbles my parents and I were accustomed to having, over topics ranging from my hair to my politics, vanished for a while; seeing their baby boy looking like a piece of raw meat, laying motionless in a hospital bed with tubes everywhere, they could only count their blessings that I had come out of the whole thing alive. For another, I myself learned that being at death's door does give you some new things to think about.

The second crisis happened at the end of my senior year, when the founder of the Misty Mountain Maulers, who had gone on to MIT, where he became a basketball star, prankster, and budding intellectual in good standing, died, wasted, from cancer. The five remaining Maulers were thrown for a loop. We would still have our Viking Feasts, still play ball into the night, still drop sarcastic lines, and so on. But things were different. For a good while afterward, I was aimless, a kind of nomad, moving through people and places and things without quite being there. Much of that period is difficult to recall.

When I got to college the following fall, I took a few interesting courses, made some new friends, had a couple of short-lived but entertaining relationships, and spent a great deal of time listening to extremely loud music in the poster-strewn dorm I lived in with my frazzled roommate, who, rumor had it, had ingested so many powerful mind-altering substances that his hair and beard had just plain stopped growing. He did eventually go on to graduate school at Harvard to study architecture, so apparently he managed to retain some functioning brain cells beneath all that hair, frozen in its tracks, but he was quite a piece of work. In any case, things were okay back then, but as I can see now, in hindsight, just okay. I missed too many classes, which was a big mistake; I got so-so grades and was actually relieved about it; and I really didn't connect at all to what I was learning. Part of the problem had to do with the courses I was taking. As a fledgling psychology major, eager to plumb the depths of the human condition and perhaps give some form to the strange and confusing world within me, I was disappointed to find myself in classes with hundreds of people, often reading tedious textbooks, taught by boring professors or inexperienced graduate assistants who seemed more interested in playing with their laboratory toys than they were in exploring the inner recesses of Being. But another part of the problem was me. The D– I received on my first college essay had put some fear into me, and it was a bit disconcerting to try to learn the contents of an entire course in a night or two. But none of this had been enough to shock me into getting serious about school. So, the first year was okay, but again, just okay. Something was missing, and I could feel it in my gut even then.

Sophomore year was different. First, I had met someone—a free-thinking but serious anthropology major, interested in poetry and dance—who helped me get some of my priorities straight. In addition, I found myself gravitating toward an intellectual crowd, for whom Eastern philosophy and modern fiction were often the topics of the day. A group of us moved off campus the second semester of that year; as far as we were concerned, we had exhausted the dormitory scene and decided that living in a house together, communally, was a far more cool thing to do. We were all remarkably proud of that house, and this despite the fact that it was a dump. I, in particular, was so proud that I immediately invited my parents up for the weekend, so they could behold their independent, intellectually cutting-edge son's wonderful new abode. My mother remained quiet, in a "This is nice, dear" sort of mode. My father, on the other hand, was horrified. Sleeping on an old mattress on the floor of my bedroom, which I had (unconsciously) painted the color of Howard Johnson's—orange ceiling, turquoise walls— was one thing. The living room furniture ("Oh, the people down the street were throwing it out, Dad") was another. My bearded, shoeless, yogi-like housemates, wafting about like so much vapor, was another still. My parents fled as soon as they possibly could. So much for pride in one's new abode.

But something strange and wonderful happened that spring, when my dad picked me up at school to take me home for summer vacation. The two of us were alone in a car for four hours—something that had never happened before. And he and I *talked* with one another, about college, about life, about ourselves, two men, father and son, making up for the strains and silences of a lifetime. He didn't tell me straightaway—he was never given to that sort of direct disclosure—but right then and there he let me know, as best he could, that I was all right, even with my shaggy mane, weird friends, and dilapidated house. He could tell, I suppose, that I was in the process of heading somewhere and that I would probably turn out all right. When I was off working at a camp that summer I even received a letter from him, in which he basically said that it had been a pleasure to meet me and that he was confident that things were, in their own way, progressing nicely. He couldn't possibly have had any idea at all about what I would do in the world, concretely. I didn't either. But there were hints that it might be *something*. I do wish that he could have seen what; not unlike my brother with the jailbird fantasy of my future, he probably would have been quite surprised.

It was only a brief while after receiving that letter, that seal of approval, that I received a call in the camp's kitchen from my oldest brother telling me that dad was gone. He had been at my uncle's pool, swimming, and his heart had seized on him and wrenched his life away, just like that. Thirty-five years ago, this man I loved and in some ways barely knew, my father, who had just yesterday, or what seemed like it, sat and talked with me for the first time, who had uttered words that would echo through the years, speaking what I came to think of as "the presence of what is missing" (Freeman, 2002c). The ride home: this "incident," such as it was, may appear entirely too fleeting and undefined to serve as a focal point for an exploration of hindsight. I cannot recall the details of our conversation, formative though it seems to have been. I cannot remember which car we drove or which route we took home or where we stopped to eat. It is all a blur; there is almost nothing. And some of what I do recall is, in a certain sense, impossible. As I look back, I can see the two of us in the front seat; I can see myself turning my head his way, leaning toward him. He doesn't quite look back, his eyes remain on the road, but he's fully there, doing what he can to connect with me. It is as if this picture is taken from the back seat, off to the side, or somewhere near there. There's the steady hum of the road underneath, and the scenery flashes by, like time. Something is condensed in this scene, something unspeakable, has raised it to the level of a kind of mythic moment, a *founding* moment, that ended up inaugurating an entirely different way of thinking about him, me, and the relationship between us.

An important fact ought to be acknowledged here. Had my dad not died, suddenly and inexplicably, two months later, this incident I have been at pains to recount would have had far less power and privilege in my history. It may simply have been a nice ride home, surprising and gratifying for the talk that took place, but not much more. That's because there probably would have been lots of other events following in its wake; life would have simply gone on, like the flashing scenery, and that ride home would have receded like so many other scenes, falling backward into the past. But life didn't simply go on; it came to a screeching halt. And as a result, the ride home, even amid its fleetingness, its lack of definition and clarity, has come to loom large in my memory. It has become a monument, a commemorative psychic edifice that I can sometimes enter.

PRESENCE AND ABSENCE

It has become common knowledge that memory, far from reproducing past experience as it was, is constructive and imaginative, maybe even fictive, in its workings. Along these lines, it might therefore be suggested that I myself have created a fiction of sorts surrounding that ride home, transforming what might otherwise have been just another event into something extra important and meaningful—foundational, as I called it. In one sense, this is quite right: without my own imaginative reworking of what happened that fine spring day, without my desire to tell it this way rather than that, it would indeed have been just another event. For all I know, mothers and fathers and their college-age children were all around us, littering the highways, talking with one another, making contact. Isn't that all we were doing?

Interpretations proliferate at this point. It could be that, in order for me to fend off the grim reality of my father having died without our ever really having the opportunity to make contact, I had to somehow convince myself that we did: after 20 years, something had happened, a breakthrough; boy, was I lucky. In this case, of course, much of what I have told you would deserve to be called illusory, more the product of a wish than a reality. Similarly, perhaps I have merely devised a means, through this yarn, to assuage some of my guilt and shame over the fact that, at the time of his death, I had done decidedly less than my brothers to make him proud. Maybe I had to convince myself that he could see that I was finally getting it together, that I had some promise and potential; to admit that he had seen nothing of the sort would have been too painful, too wasteful. Each of these interpretations presumes that I had somehow foisted meaning onto that car ride, that I had used it as a means of ensuring that there was—or that there appeared to be—some redeeming value to our lives together. I could have chosen any one of a number of things to serve in this role; not unlike the way dreams seem to work, according to Freud at any rate, maybe I just latched on to this particular scene because it somehow allowed me to do what was necessary to carry on with some measure of self-affirmation: I think I can make something of that car ride . . . .

All this is possible. But there is another way entirely of understanding what has been done here. The fact is, I don't really take much solace from that ride home. I'm certainly glad it happened, and in that sense I do feel "lucky." But that incident, as I suggested a short while ago, is as much about what was, and is, missing as anything else. It is about what was missing from our relationship. There could have been so much—in a way, we proved it in that car—and yet there wasn't nearly enough. I can still feel the presence of what we missed together. It is also about what is missing now. It's been many years since that ride home, and in so much of what I have done since that time, particularly those things I might have been able to share with him or that might have made him proud or happy, he is right there, missing. Strictly speaking, it's not so much *him* I miss, in the sense of a present being. Rather, I feel the presence of his absence. This in itself might serve to correct the idea that memory deals only with what has actually happened, with "events," once there, now gone. Memory also deals with what didn't happen and what couldn't happen and what will never happen.

There is another way still of fleshing out this idea of the presence of what is missing, and it is here that I turn once more to the idea of *poiesis*. It is sometimes said that poetry seeks to make present what is absent in our ordinary, everyday encounters with the world. Or, to put the matter more philosophically, it is a making-present of the world in its absence; it is thus seen to provide a kind of "supplement" to ordinary experience, serving to draw out features of the world that would otherwise go unnoticed. But a kind of puzzle is at work here. If it is assumed that these features go *totally* unnoticed and that absence is essentially complete, then poetry can be nothing more than the fashioning of illusions, replacing absence with presence. Not unlike what was said earlier regarding that view of memory, which speaks of foisting meanings onto the past, it would have to be considered one more defensive maneuver, one more attempt to fend off meaninglessness. This is possible too: it could be that the meaning of poems, like the meaning of my ride home with my dad, is merely a matter of wishes, that things could be other than the way they are.

But it could also be that absence is *not* complete and that the world of ordinary experience bears within its absence a certain presence, a limited presence, which the poet, in turn, must try to bring to light. The poet Seamus Heaney has spoken of the "redressing" effect of poetry in this context, which "comes from its being a glimpsed alternative, a revelation of potential that is denied or constantly threatened by circumstances" (1995, p. 4).

I also spoke earlier of the idea of "recuperative disclosure," the notion being that poetry, like hindsight, seeks to explicate what is there, in the world, and thereby rescue it from the forgetful oblivion that so often characterizes our relatedness to things. In a sense, you could say that poetry deals with what's not there and there at the same time. From one angle, it's about what is absent in presence; it's about what's often missing from our ordinary experience of things by virtue of its being "denied" or "threatened by circumstances." From another angle, it's about what's present in absence, the existence of a certain potential, "waiting" to be disclosed. Along the lines being drawn here, there is nothing intrinsically defensive or illusory at all about poems. On the contrary: they may very well serve as vehicles of disclosure and revelation, not so much "giving" meaning to experience as allowing it to emerge.

The same basic thing may be said about hindsight. A short while ago, you will recall, I flirted with the possibility that the ride home with my dad, ordinary as it was in many ways, might simply be serving as an occasion for me to do some psychological patch-up work. I also acknowledged that, had that ride home not been followed by death, its story might have been told quite differently. Indeed, it may not have been told at all. But what my dad's death seemed to do was activate the poetic function of memory, such that I would return to that ride home and try to disclose what was there, waiting. The incident itself, as an historical event, was filled with a kind of diffuse, unspecified potential. It could have been played out in a wide variety of different ways, from the most ordinary and unmemorable all the way to the most extraordinary and memorable. It all depends on what follows. The reason the balance has in this case been tipped to the latter is clear enough. If only that ride could have remained in its ordinariness, pleasant and good, father and son, going home for the summer. But it has become filled with an urgency that will always remain. This urgency is not something I put there. Rather, it is something that exists in the very fabric of this story I have been trying to tell. Writing, of this sort, can be strange. Even though I have tried here to "create" something—an image, you could call it, of a significant incident—there is no feeling at all that this image is merely a weakened replica of the real or that it is merely imaginary. Recall Bonnefoy's earlier words: "this world which cuts itself off from the world," he told us, "seems to the person who creates it not only more satisfying than the first but also more real" (1989, p. 164). The situation is a fragile and delicate one. "In the midst of this absence, something like a voice which persists" (p. 167). The ride home, etched first in memory, now in writing, speaks in this voice. Nothing is more real.

FATE AND FEAR

The story continues. As fate would have it, the very next year, there was a complete turn-around in my college experience. There was one course in psychology, another in philosophy; they were about fundamental questions of meaning and value, in life and in art. And suddenly, the world of ideas seized me, took me by storm: the power and the beauty of what could be thought and said and written and painted let me know for the first time that there were some truly worthwhile things to do. I had finally become a student. How ironic that it should have happened within months of that awful summer day. Or, maybe not. It is difficult to say.

Given the way my father died, at poolside, it is strange that my memory of him often turns to our times together in the water, in the ocean especially, playing in the waves. He somehow seemed more at home there than anywhere else, and he seemed closer to us too. People say that my dad and I have a great deal in common. I look more like him than either of my brothers do. When I went to a memorial service a while ago and encountered some long-lost relatives, several were taken aback, in shock almost: "Oh my God, it's Bernie . . . ." "You look more and more like your father . . . ." "He's the spitting image; only he has a neck and Bernie didn't . . . ." (When my father was at his heaviest, his head rested squarely on his shoulders.) I also share his moods and mood-swings; there are lots of good times and lots of laughs, but rage and sullenness are always a short step away. I also like good food and drink and nice clothes and a number of other things my father had been drawn to. Who knows? Maybe in the absence of his being there, I took in what I could of his desires and made them my own. And I've always loved playing in the water, especially with my two daughters, Brenna and Justine. They would dive off my shoulders and glide through my legs when they were little. I would swim under-water, unseen and unheard, and take them by surprise. *Don't!* they would scream. *More.* Sometimes we would just hold one another, gathering as much warmth as we could. These were moments of fullness and presence and, at the same time, sadness and brevity: nothing lasts forever. Oh, if he could have known those two girls, his granddaughters, playing in the water, glis-tening in the sun like jewels.

As I noted in the first chapter, one of them, the older one, gave me quite a scare some years ago. A couple of days before my departure for a conference, our (then) 12-year-old daughter, Brenna, had woken up and was barely able to speak. She was congested, her chest hurt, and she was a little flushed. It turned out to be a case of pneumonia, viral supposedly. Seeing one's child extremely ill can be very tough. At the time, Brenna was a bit frail and pale to begin with. And seeing her huddled under her blankets, her face peeking out, fixed on the TV, eyes glazed, murmuring a faint hello . . . it's hard not to have this kind of scene break your heart.

It's not as if I had been a perpetual mess for the two days that followed the diagnosis. The doctor didn't seem too concerned and, by and large, it was life as usual—permeated by an extra load of worry (not to mention guilt over my impending departure for the conference, leaving my suffering family behind) but not radically different than most other days. The next night, however, my wife and I were watching the 10 o'clock news and we learned that a 10-year-old girl, from Boston (less than an hour away), had suddenly died. She had had flu-like symptoms and been taken to the hospital just a day earlier—where nothing out of the ordinary had been diagnosed—and 24 hours later she was, mysteriously, given the speed with which her young body had been ravaged, gone. Her beautiful smiling face was in a little inset on the TV screen as the newscaster reviewed her fate. It was probably one of those photos they take of kids in school, where they wear their Sunday dresses or their clip-on ties.

She had apparently contracted a virulent form of bacterial pneumonia. In another child's body, the TV doctor explained, there might hardly have been a problem. And it was extremely rare for anything like this occur. Sometimes this sort of catastrophe is just a matter of sheer bad luck, the doctor went on to say: a receptive body meets up with a dreadful bacterium, and, in a matter of hours, a little girl, thoroughly alive just a day before, is dead. But it was extremely rare, the doctor reiterated. And it was *bacterial,* not *viral.* The facts of the matter aside, this was not a good piece of news to watch the night before leaving for the dry plains of Lubbock, Texas, where the conference was to be held. How exactly did our doctor know that what Brenna had was viral and not bacterial? And how did we know that she didn't have one of those terrible rare bodies, which might serve as an all too willing host to an unspeakably hostile germ?

The next morning she looked a little better (or so I told myself). At least she didn't seem to have taken a turn for the worse. It wasn't that intense a morning, in fact, and I have no interest in making it any more dramatic than it was. Things changed, however, for a few moments, as I looked at my wife and Brenna standing in the doorway, looking at me presumably—although I actually didn't know if they could see me behind the smoky glass of the limo van that would take me to the airport. When I waved, they didn't wave back. There they were, the two of them, one taller and ruddy, the other shorter and pasty, soon to recede from view. What would be the meaning of that morning, that picture, etched in my mind's eye? The fact is, I did not know. I *could* not know—not, that is, until further experiences came along and gave it a more definite meaning. This again bespeaks the limits of present consciousness. The issue here, however, is not shortsightedness. Nor is it the absence of that temporal distance which would allow one to see, from afar, contours of a moment that one simply cannot see when that moment is transpiring. The issue is simply one of *time:* without knowing the ending of this story-in-the-making, there was no way at all to glean the significance of that parting. When I left, everything was wide open, and I could only hope that the story I would eventually tell had a happy ending—unexciting though it would have to be. The story was contingent on the future, on what would happen over the next couple of days.

"Consider what happens," the philosopher Gabriel Marcel (1950) has written,

> when we tell our friends the very simplest story, the story, say, of some journey we have made. The story of a journey is told by

someone who has made the journey, from beginning to end, and who inevitably sees his earlier experiences during the journey as coloured by his later experiences. For our final impression of what the journey turned out to be like cannot but react on our memories of our first impression of what the journey *was going to be like*. But when we were actually making the journey, or rather beginning to make it, these first impressions were, on the contrary, held quivering like a compass needle by our anxious expectations of everything that was still to come. (p. 192)

This does not mean that present experience is completely indeterminate or meaningless. What it does mean is that the meaning and significance of that experience will change, to a greater or lesser extent, as a function of what the future brings. They are thus transformed, via hindsight, our "anxious expectations," or fears, or fantasies having been superseded in line with what has transpired since. An incident, its potential inchoate, becomes an episode; a narrative-to-be becomes a narrative.

Here, then, we return to a question posed earlier: Are we falsifying the past by projecting meanings onto it that don't rightly belong there? Possibly. But not necessarily. What we are doing is remembering and narrating, which means situating the experiences of the past in relation to what has happened since, as understood, and reunderstood, from the present, via hindsight. The way most memory theorists frame this state of affairs is to say that our memories are heavily influenced by our present situation—by outcome knowledge; by various external sources; by our interests, wishes, and desires. Michael Ross and Anne Wilson (2000), for instance, note that "individuals' self-concepts, beliefs, and implicit theories influence their recollections" (p. 237). Likewise, you may recall, Daniel Schacter and

Elaine Scarry (2000), in their reflections on "retrospective bias," try to show that "one's memories of past experiences can be influenced by one's current beliefs" (p. 3). This seems to make sense. Nevertheless, I would frame this set of issues differently. The fact is, these theorists' formulations—however "constructivist" they may be—continue to insist on the separability of memory from individuals' self-concepts, beliefs, implicit theories, and so on. But these, I would argue, are a part of memory itself. I shall have much more to say about this issue in Chapter 4, when we explore more deeply the profound ways in which external sources of information—from other people, books, movies, and more—become part of the very substance and texture of memory. For the time being, let me return to the uncertain situation of my pulling away in that van, wife and sickly daughter slowly fading from view, still, not even waving. What *was* this? What would it *be?* If only we could know! But of course, we cannot. It is not for nothing that fate and fear so often go hand in hand.

HINDSIGHT AND INSIGHT

As I thought more about the episode with my daughter, I began to link it up, tentatively, and cautiously, with my father. It could be, I realized, that there was some connection—that there *is* some connection, psychical in nature—between how I responded to her as the van pulled away and what had happened that fateful summer: it could be, it can always be, the last time. That early wound may be even fresher and more powerful than I sometimes assume, and has created, on the fringes of my consciousness, a certain fragility in regard to how I think and feel about people I care for. I have framed this in terms of "what might have led to what," almost in a causal way. But the dimension of hindsight is key. Only in virtue of the later event was it possible to think anew about the earlier one and about the possible relationship between the two.

A "possible relationship": What exactly are we talking about here? If one were to speak of causation at all, it would be imperative to recognize that it is a retrospectively posited form of causation: it is the effect (my extremely fearful response to my daughter's illness), we might say, that instigates the location of a possible cause (my father's sudden and untimely death), the possible relationship between the two being a function of (possible) *insight via hindsight*. I say "possible" because, strictly speaking—that is, speaking according to the causal or probabilistic principles ordinarily associated with scientific reason—I could not possibly *know* for certain whether the relationship being posited actually obtains. All this means, however, is that this possible relationship, fashioned through the imaginative labor of hindsight, is of a different order of "reason" than that which is ordinarily associated with science. On one level, the kind of reason being considered is poetic in nature, having to do precisely with that process of "making sense of" that we considered at the beginning of this chapter. One could also speak of a *hermeneutical* dimension: In dealing with a possible relationship of this sort, I am irrevocably enmeshed within the circle of interpretation, bringing to bear all that I know and am upon the "text" at hand.[2]

---

[2] Hermeneutics refers to the theory and practice of interpreting texts, and is especially concerned with the relationship between interpreter and text as well as the circular movement between part and whole that characterizes the interpretive process. For notable examples in philosophy, see Gadamer, 1975, 1976; Heidegger, 1962 [1927]; Ricoeur, 1976, 1981a. In psychology and related social sciences, see Messer, Sass, & Woolfolk, 1988; Packer & Addison, 1989; Rabinow & Sullivan, 1979, 1987.

But the texts about which I have been speaking differ from those on our bookshelves. In dealing with works of literature, there exist objects (i.e., books) outside the perimeter of the interpreting self. Determining the nature of these objects is itself a constructive act; and for this reason, some theorists have gone so far as to say that readers actually construct the very texts they read. This caveat notwithstanding, few, presumably, would quarrel with the notion that there is *something* there, with pages and words, prior to the entry of any given interpreter, and that these pages and words circumscribe the kinds of constructions that are ultimately made.

But in the case of memories, and possible relationships between memories, what is actually there? In this context, we are dealing with texts that we ourselves have fashioned. I try to make sense of *my* past, and you yours. But this past, far from existing outside the perimeter of the interpreting self, in the manner of the literary text, is itself something of my own making, my own *imagining*. "What memory 'sees,'" memoirist Patricia Hampl has written, "it must regard through the image-making faculty of mind" (1999, p. 224). Memory is a making-present of what is absent—that ride home, that morning in the van, both now long gone. In dealing with such events, therefore—remembered events, filtered, inevitably, through the prism of my present world—I am both interpreting and creating, finding and making, at the same time: I discover a possible relationship between remembered events through imagining the possibility, and in so doing I refashion my past. There thus emerges a connection between my father and my daughter that wasn't quite visible before.

How, then, shall we make sense of connections of this sort? Generally, we have two options. The first looks essentially forward in time, perhaps making use of the discourse of causation: from this perspective, the first experience "led to," or even caused, the second. I couldn't have *predicted* the latter, my daughter's illness, from the former, my father's death; it was wholly unanticipated, and its emergence was a matter of fate. But feeling what I did over my daughter's illness and then looking backward to discern its possible sources, it became clear that my earlier experience, saturated in fear and loss, had somehow "brought about" the later one. This first option, which imagines that one can somehow translate the backward movement of history into the forward movement of causation, is problematic, not least because it attributes causative/predictive power to events and experiences that only come to have the significance they do by virtue of what happens subsequently, which may be utterly fortuitous.[3] Its model of time is the line, moving ever forward, and it is inadequate to much of the human realm.

The second option is, in a sense, the inverted image of the first: it's not the past that determines the present, but vice versa, the supposition being that positing connections of this sort entails imposing meaning on the past as a function of what one knows about the present. Here, therefore, the movement is backward rather than forward. Thinking in this second way serves as a valuable corrective to the first. In highlighting the significance of the present in the fashioning of the past, one acknowledges more fully not only the hermeneutical dimension of hindsight but also the retrospective dimension: one is interpreting, making-sense-of the "text" of the past from the vantage point of the present, and is discerning meanings that have only become available in hindsight. It is this retrospective dimension,

[3] See Freeman, 1984, 1993; also Brockmeier, 2000, 2001.

it may be argued, that renders hindsight so suspect. It cannot, and does not, represent the past as it was; the present inevitably intrudes. Consequently (the argument goes), some measure of falsification must occur. There is only a story, a fiction, wrought out of the designs and desires of the narrator. This view, I have also suggested, is equally problematic.

Consider once more the ride home with my father. I talked about its meaning and significance, the fact of it having become a monument in my history. From the first perspective, that ride had to have borne within it a certain determinative energy and potential; it somehow had to "lead" to what subsequently happened in me. But this cannot be; for what subsequently happened in me was itself a function of an utterly unanticipated death. The ride, therefore, acquired the meaning and significance it did *retroactively*, owing to that dreadful event and its reverberations in time. From the second perspective, the ride would likely be seen as a kind of blank screen, onto which I would eventually project meaning and significance. I bought into a story line, perhaps; I felt the need to adorn the past with my own fantastic needs and wishes, thereby rendering the present a bit more tolerable. If the first account gives too much credit to the determinative power of events, the latter gives too little.

We are neither the archeologists of our histories, unearthing what had been there all along, nor their inventors, fashioning them *ex nihilo*, out of nothing. Not unlike poets, we are creators, fashioning and refashioning the work that is our lives, through narrative, via hindsight, in such a way as to disclose the potential that experience bears within it and that will be released, in this direction or that, depending on what happens later on. The movement at hand is neither strictly forward nor strictly backward but a kind of poetically figured spiral, a dialectical shuttling back and forth, issuing from the imaginative labor required to make sense of experience. As death shows us, loud and clear, "you can't turn back the clock." There thus remains a quite real sense in which time moves irrevocably forward. This is what I referred to earlier as the time of clocks. But, as I also suggested, we live in the time not only of clocks, in which events come ticking along, following one another in their sameness, but also of narrative. It makes sense that that car ride home has acquired the meaning and significance it has. And it also makes sense that there should have emerged in my mind a connection between my father and daughter that hadn't been visible until she fell ill. This sense issues from the narrative imagination, and it is, I believe, uniquely a part of the fashioning and refashioning not only of our pasts but also our very selves.

THREE

MORAL LATENESS

THE DANGERS OF LOOKING BACKWARD

Some of the dangers of looking backward over the landscape of the personal past are well known. As Michel Leiris notes in his autobiography, *Manhood* (1984 [1939]), the past has been reconstructed "according to my recollections, adding the observation of what I have subsequently become and comparing these later elements with those earlier ones my memory supplies. Such a method has its dangers," Leiris writes, "for who knows if I am not attributing to these recollections a meaning they never had, charging them after the fact with an affective value which the real events they refer to utterly lacked—in short, resuscitating this past in a misleading manner?" (p. 22). As I suggested in the previous chapter, there are times when this "charging" after-the-fact is justifiable: through the narrative imagination, what happened earlier can come to occupy a place in an evolving narrative that confers upon it a meaning and significance it did not, and could not, have at the time.

But there are more troubling instances of this process as well, ones that are based, for instance, on a refusal to see the past for what it was and that result in an effort to paper it over and render it innocuous. This mode of looking backward can culminate not only in depicting the past in a "misleading" manner but in one that is utterly false. This itself suggests something vitally important about both hindsight and the narratives that issue from it: impossible though it may be to tell the absolute truth of one's story—the interpretive nature of narrative reflection patently precludes it—it is perfectly possible to *lie*; that is, to tell stories of the past that simply fly in the face of what is known to be true.

I shall be exploring several variants of this process shortly via Primo Levi's *The Drowned and the Saved* (1989). He notes, for example, that it was difficult for the perpetrators of heinous crimes during the Holocaust to see the past for what it was, and for obvious reason: to do so would be to avow their culpability, to implicate themselves in the evil they had wrought. So it is that many of them had crafted sanitized stories, stories that had been carefully—even if, in some instances, unwittingly—cleansed, purged of the dirty realities of which they had been a part. This can be psychologically valuable, at least for a time. The stories we tell about the personal past are intimately related to our identities, our sense of who and what we are, in the eyes of others as well as ourselves.[1] As long as I can tell a tolerably good story, I can remain a tolerably good person. Or so it appears.

A quite different kind of danger is involved in looking backward as well, one that is essentially the opposite of what has just been considered. Here, I refer again to the fact that one can look

[1] For works in psychology exploring the relationship between narrative and identity, see Brockmeier & Carbaugh, 2001; Fivush & Hayden, 2003; Freeman, 1993; McAdams, 1997; McAdams, Josselson, & Lieblich, 2006. In philosophy, see Flanagan, 1996; Ricoeur, 1992; also, in literature, Eakin, 2008.

back upon an earlier experience or set of experiences and find things in them that either could not or would not be seen at the time. It is not only the past that can be papered over and falsified but the present: in the midst of my anger or horror or weakness, I can convince myself, quite spontaneously, that what I am doing is justified, even right, good. But then, later on, after the dust has cleared, I may see it all anew, and with painful clarity. The danger in this case may be nothing less than the truth itself. As Primo Levi's recounting of some of his own behavior as a concentration camp prisoner will show, this truth can hurt; for in admitting into memory the unsanitized story of the past one also may be forced to admit the unclean nature of one's very being.

The idea of moral "lateness" introduced in the first chapter assumes a fever pitch in this context: having become aware after the fact of the full measure of his own culpability and complicity—or having come to believe it—Levi sees himself as beyond forgiveness, beyond redemption. Some evidence in fact suggests that Levi may have taken his own life due, in part, to this very conviction. For present purposes, whether this is true or not is largely immaterial. For, as Levi's words show, with radiant and awful clarity, there is no question but that he had been tortured by what hindsight had revealed, about him and about humanity. How tragically ironic: while Nazi perpetrators could bask in the glow of their own illusions and lies, their victims could be victimized once more, burned by the late-breaking truths disclosed through hindsight. The good news, such as it is, is that hindsight serves in instances like these as a hopeful reminder of our moral capacities and potentials. Looking backward, we can often see the errors of our ways. But of course this seeing has arrived late on the scene, and its very lateness in coming also bespeaks some of the profound limits of moral life.

SANITIZED STORIES

In one chapter of *The Drowned and the Saved,* "The Memory of the Offense," Levi calls attention to some of the aforementioned dangers inherent in the process of remembering, particularly when tied to things one would rather forget. "The memories which lie within us," he writes, "are not carved in stone; not only do they tend to become erased as the years go by, but often they change, or even grow, by incorporating extraneous features." Levi goes on to identify some of the mechanisms known to falsify memory under particular conditions: "traumas, not only cerebral ones; interference from other 'competitive' memories; abnormal conditions of consciousness; repressions; blockages" (p. 23). But "even under normal conditions," he adds,

> a slow degradation is at work, an obfuscation of outlines, a so to speak physiological oblivion, which few memories resist. Doubtless one may discern here one of the great powers of nature, the same that degrades order into disorder, youth into old age, and extinguishes life in death. Certainly practice . . . keeps memories fresh and alive in the same manner in which a muscle often used remains efficient, but it is also true that a memory evoked too often, and expressed in the form of a story, tends to become fixed in a stereotype, in a form tested by experience, crystallized, perfected, adorned, installing itself in the place of the raw memory and growing at its expense. (p. 24)

It is not clear whether memory is ever quite as "raw" as Levi makes it out to be; as Sir Frederic Bartlett showed long ago in his classic book *Remembering* (1995 [1932]), memory, particularly of the sort being considered here, generally involves reconstruction, the refashioning and "rewriting" of the past. Be that as it may, Levi is surely right to call attention to the fact that a memory "evoked too often" frequently leads to the formation of stories that grow stereotypical, becoming ever more schematized and conventionalized over the course of time.[2]

Levi's main project in this chapter, however, is to identify those factors that can alter the "mnemonic record" (p. 24), especially among those who have a vested psychic interest in doing so. When asked why they had committed such horrendous crimes during the Nazi era, many of the perpetrators offered similar answers: "I did it because I was ordered to; others (my superiors) have committed acts worse than mine; in view of the upbringing I received, and the environment in which I lived, I could not have acted differently; had I not done it, another would have done it even more harshly in my place" (p. 26). As Levi notes, the first reaction of many who hear about such justifications is revulsion: "they lie," it is often said; "they cannot believe they will be believed, they cannot see the imbalance between their excuses and the enormity of pain and death they have caused" (p. 26). But it is not so simple, Levi insists. There are indeed those who have resorted to outright lies in their attempt to save their own skins,

> but more numerous are those who weigh anchor, move off, momentarily or forever, from genuine memories, and fabricate for themselves a convenient reality. The past is a burden to them; they feel repugnance for things done or suffered and tend to replace them with others. The substitution may begin in full awareness, with an invented scenario, mendacious, restored, but

---

[2] See especially Schachtel's classic chapter "On Memory and Childhood Amnesia," from *Metamorphosis*, 1959.

less painful than the real one; they repeat the description to others but also to themselves, and the distinction between true and false progressively loses its contours, and man ends by fully believing the story he has told so many times and continues to tell, polishing and retouching here and there the details which are least credible or incongruous or incompatible with the acquired picture of historically accepted events: initial bad faith has become good faith. The silent transition from falsehood to self-deception is useful: anyone who lies in good faith is better off. He recites his part better, is more easily believed by the judge, the historian, the reader, his wife, and his children. (p. 27)

And the process goes on and on. "The further events fade into the past, the more the construction of convenient truth grows and is perfected" (p. 27). Hence "the typical case of someone who, accustomed to lying in public, ends by lying in private, too, to himself as well, and building for himself a comforting truth which allows him to live in peace" (p. 28). Whether such a person can live in *real* peace remains an open question; one wonders about his or her dream life, or about those fleeting moments when, despite one's best efforts, truth reveals its ugly head. Can "initial bad faith," as Levi had put it, truly become "good faith"? It is difficult to say. Levi's main point stands in any case: by all indications, the consolatory designs of memory, and story, seemed to work wonders for many of those in need.

Alongside the process of reconstructing the past to fit one's psychic needs is the process of suppression: "Here, too," Levi acknowledges, "the borderline between good and bad faith can be vague; behind the 'I don't know' and the 'I do not remember' that one hears in courtrooms there is sometimes the precise intent to lie, but at other times it is a fossilized lie, rigidified in a formula. The rememberer has decided not to remember and has succeeded: by dint of denying its existence, he has expelled the harmful memory as one expels an excretion or a parasite" (p. 30). Also effective is the process of denying entry altogether to those memories that might, someday, serve to disturb the peace of one's illusions. So it was that some of the *Einsatzcommandos*, "who behind the front lines in Russia machine-gunned civilians beside common graves which the victims themselves had been forced to dig, were given all the liquor they wanted so that the massacre would be blurred by drunkenness" (p. 31). There was virtually no memory to be had in such circumstances; reality would remain hidden, beclouded, known only to those keeping the killers in good supply.

According to Levi, "the entire history of the brief 'millennial Reich' can be reread as a war against memory, an Orwellian falsification of memory, falsification of reality, negation of reality" (p. 31). In many ways, the picture of memory he presents here is a familiar one. As suggested already, memory often becomes highly schematized and conventionalized with the passage of time. What also happens is that the memory in question becomes subservient to narrative, which has its own conventional, culture-specific norms, rules, and expectations.[3] Add to this the dynamic dimension about which Levi speaks—the need to protect or defend, to offer a story, to others and to oneself, that has some justification to it—and the entire situation becomes that much more dangerous and pernicious. From this perspective, therefore, hindsight is seen to entail a dissolution or deformation of past realities. As one moves away from the experiences in

[3] See, e.g., Bruner, 1990.

question, the picture becomes vaguer, blurrier, more susceptible to standardized—and sanitized—renditions.

Consider the metaphor of the aerial view: When sitting in an airplane on the ground, everything outside seems sharp and well-delineated; once high in the air, the concrete things you saw on the ground become shapes, patterns, generic designs. You can also see things that could not be seen on the ground, or you may see familiar things in a different way. Depending on the scenery, it can be quite beautiful. The same is true of hindsight; there is much that can be appreciated, anew, from afar—that ride home, for instance, with my dad. This is one of hindsight's great gifts. But it doesn't always work this way. The fact is, there is much that can be seen in retrospect that boggles the mind and shatters the spirit. Let us turn now to a particularly telling case of just this sort of reversal of fortune.

The Narrative Abyss

As Levi writes in his chapter on "Shame," also from *The Drowned and the Saved* (1989),

> A certain fixed image has been proposed innumerable times, consecrated by literature and poetry, and picked up by the cinema: "the quiet before the storm," when all hearts rejoice. . . . The disease runs its course and health returns. To deliver us from imprisonment "our boys," the liberators, arrive just in time, with waving flags; the soldier returns and again finds his family and peace. (p. 70)

The story is almost archetypal in its imagery. According to Levi, however, it is largely illusory. "In the majority of cases," he continues, the hour of liberation was neither joyful nor lighthearted. For most it occurred against a tragic background of destruction, slaughter, and suffering. Just as they felt they were again becoming men, that is, responsible, the sorrows of men returned: the sorrow of the dispersed or lost family; the universal suffering all around; their own exhaustion, which seemed definitive, past cure; the problems of a life to begin all over again amid the rubble, often alone. Not "pleasure the son of misery," but misery the son of misery. (p. 71)

It's true that there was "full, authentic joy" for some of the liberated. There were also "those who have the virtue and the privilege of extracting . . . instants of happiness . . . as though they were extracting pure gold from dross." There were also those who managed to replace "genuine memory" with conventionalized stories not unlike the mythicized ones enshrined in the cinema. Whatever the reality of their past situation, these people somehow managed to tell about it in an upbeat, even joyful way. Perhaps they were thankful for the fact that their narratives, illusory though they might have been, had essentially obliterated the pastness of the past; there was hardly a reason to return to that particular form of presence.

But then there were those like Levi himself, for whom this very notion of presence, tied to the immediacy of experience, had to be interrogated. He cites a passage from his book *The Reawakening* (1995) that describes a quite different kind of response to liberation than any of those introduced thus far. "There had been four Russian men, armed but not against us: four messengers of peace, with rough and boyish faces beneath their heavy fur hats." But,

They did not greet us, nor did they smile; they seemed oppressed not only by compassion but by a confused restraint, which sealed their lips and bound their eyes to the funereal scene. It was that shame we knew so well, the shame that drowned us after the selections, and every time we had to watch, or submit to, some outrage: the shame the Germans did not know, that the just man experiences at another man's crime; the feeling of guilt that such a crime should exist, that it should have been introduced irrevocably into the world of things that exist, and that his will for good should have proved too weak or null, and should not have availed in defence.

So for us even the hour of liberty rang out grave and muffled, and filled our souls with joy and yet with a painful sense of pudency, so that we should have liked to wash our consciences and our memories clean from the foulness that lay upon them; and also with anguish, because we felt that this should never happen, that now nothing could ever happen good and pure enough to rub out our past, and that the scars of the outrage would be with us forever, and in the memories of those who saw it, and in the places where it occurred and in the stories that we should tell of it. (p. 16)

Hindsight, here, far from being a source of consolation, becomes instead a source of guilt and, especially, shame.

First, there was the shame of animality, as it might be called:

Coming out of the darkness, one suffered because of the reacquired consciousness of having been diminished. Not by our will, cowardice, or fault, yet nevertheless we had lived for months and years at an animal level: our days had been encumbered from dawn to dusk by hunger, fatigue, cold, and fear; and any space for reflection, reasoning, experiencing emotions was wiped out. We endured filth, promiscuity, and destitution, suffering much less than we would have suffered from such things in normal life, because our moral yardstick had changed. Furthermore, all of us had stolen: in the kitchen, the factory, the camp, in short, "from the others," from the opposing side, but it was theft nevertheless. Some (few) had fallen so low as to steal bread from their own companions. We had not only forgotten our country and our culture, but also our family, our past, the future we had imagined for ourselves, because like animals, we were confined to the present moment. (1989, p. 75)

Notice here that, for Levi, the immediate moment was something to which he and his comrades had been *confined*, indeed imprisoned. Notice, in addition, that it is only from the vantage point of the present, as he gazes back upon those terrible moments in hindsight, that Levi is able to see the enormity of the past in its full measure. It should be emphasized that he is in no way returning to the past "as it was"; to do so would be to return to that animal-like state. Instead, he is looking at the past historically, from the distant "now" of narrative reflection. And it is precisely this distance, as from above, that allows him to see, finally and tragically, the life to which he had been reduced. Those past present moments had been filled with the desperation of survival. And, far from bearing presence within them, they instead bore the deepest absence—of perspective and of humanity.

"Only at rare intervals," Levi continues, "did we come out of this condition of leveling, during the very few Sundays of rest, the fleeting minutes before falling asleep, or the fury of the air raids" (p. 75). These were "painful moments precisely because they gave us the opportunity to measure our diminishment from the outside" (p. 74). Hindsight thus presents a positive possibility here, an opportunity to "measure" one's experience from the outside, to move beyond the confines of one's blindness, or at least one's limited view of things. But it was this very possibility that yielded so much pain for Levi and others, owing to the "diminishment" that could now be seen. As Levi writes, "I believe it was precisely this turning to look back at the 'perilous water' that gave rise to so many suicides after (sometimes immediately after) Liberation." There would be "a flood of rethinking and depression" (p. 76). The all too radiant clarity of what had been would suddenly burst through the walls of consciousness. Suicides were relatively rare during imprisonment, according to Levi. Suicide entails choice, and in the camps there often *was* no choice. In addition, one had to think about other things: satisfying one's hunger, staying warm, staying alive. "Precisely because of the constant imminence of death," he writes, "there was no time to concentrate on the idea of death" (p. 76). Perhaps most centrally, however, because one was in some sense constantly being punished during imprisonment there had existed the opportunity for the regular expiation of one's guilt—which, on Levi's account, is one of the prime motives for suicide. Once this external punishment was removed, internal punishment took over.

But why guilt, and shame? Levi's first attempt to answer this question is a tragic one: psychically speaking, "if there is punishment, there must have been guilt" (p. 76). But the tragedy deepens: "When all was over," he writes, "the awareness emerged that we had not done anything, or not enough, against the system in which we had been absorbed" (p. 76). Levi, of course, realizes that much had been working against them: "Malnutrition, despoilment, and other physical discomforts, which it is so easy and economically advantageous to provoke and at which the Nazis were masters, are rapidly destructive and paralyze before destroying, all the more so when they are preceded by years of segregation, humiliation, maltreatment, forced migration, laceration of family ties, rupture of contact with the rest of the world" (p. 77). Rationally speaking, then, there wasn't much reason for excessive guilt or shame. Yet they nevertheless emerged, corrosive, and indeed, for many, deadly. Levi and his comrades would occasionally witness the strength of resistors, some of whom were hanged publicly. "This is a thought that then barely grazed us," Levi writes, "but that returned 'afterward': you too could have, you certainly should have. And this is a judgment that the survivor believes he sees in the eyes of those (especially the young) who listen to his stories and judge with facile hindsight, or who perhaps feel cruelly repelled. Consciously or not, he feels accused and judged, compelled to justify and defend himself" (pp. 77–78).

Notice here the dual workings of hindsight. Thoughts that had "barely grazed" Levi and his comrades would return, intensified and punitive: they ought to have done more. This is confirmed by the accusatory "eyes" of others who, not having been there, cannot fathom the prisoners' passivity and judge them accordingly. Notice as well the relationship between the dual workings of hindsight and the dual shaping of identity. In looking backward, what Levi sees is compounded by the internalized moral gaze of others; his own failure is public, open to inspection, or so it seems. The "could have" or "should have" of hindsight, in cases like these, thus moves beyond the confines of the individual, bearing within it a social, relational dimension. The eyes of others are within.

There could also be the shame of having failed one's fellow prisoners. "Few survivors feel guilty about having deliberately damaged, robbed, or beaten a companion," Levi notes. "Those who did so . . . block out the memory. By contrast, however, almost everybody feels guilty of having omitted to offer help" (p. 78). He goes on to tell a brief story that had continued to haunt him long after the war had ended. In August of 1944, Auschwitz was hot, and prisoners of the camp, where there was no drinkable water, were tormented by thirst. During the course of an assignment that involved clearing out rubble from a cellar, Levi had stumbled upon a two-inch pipe that contained a spigot above the floor. It looked like it might contain water, so he stretched out on the floor and had a few drops. "How much," he had asked, "can a two-inch pipe one or two meters high contain? A liter, perhaps not even that. I could have drunk it all immediately. . . . Or save a bit for the next day. Or share half of it with Alberto," his friend who was him in the cellar. "Or reveal the secret to the whole squad." He chose the third option, "that of selfishness extended to the person closest to you. . . . We drank all the water in small, avaricious gulps, changing places under the spigot, just the two of us. On the sly."

Not too long after, as they marched back to camp, Levi came upon a man named Daniele, "all gray with cement dust, his lips cracked and his eyes feverish." There was guilt: "I exchanged a look with Alberto; we understood each other immediately and hoped nobody had seen us. But Daniele had caught a glimpse of us in that strange position, supine near the wall among the rubble, and had suspected something, and then had guessed" (p. 80). Why? Daniele had asked months later. Why them and not him? Levi has his own question to wrestle with in the aftermath of the event:

Is this belated shame justified or not? I was not able to decide then and I am not able to decide even now, but shame there was and is, concrete, heavy, perennial. Daniele is dead now, but in our meetings as survivors, fraternal, affectionate, the veil of that act of omission, that unshared glass of water, stood between us, transparent, not expressed, but perceptible and "costly." (p. 81)

The question Levi is raising here is a critical one to consider, especially when addressing those aspects of hindsight that bear upon the moral realm. One may condemn oneself after the fact for lacking knowledge that one could not possibly have had. One may also condemn oneself for behaviors that could not have been avoided. In situations like these, a measure of "self-charity" is called for. Some will be able to move in this direction, others not. On the other end of the continuum, the sources of self-condemnation may be perfectly clear: you knew, and did nothing; you behaved in ways that are never excusable. And then there is the indeterminate middle, such that one may ask questions like: What didn't I know or see that I *should* have known or seen? How could I *not* have behaved in that way, given what I was facing—my thirst, my hunger, my desire to live? Undecided though Levi was about his own culpability, there would be no getting around his shame. The fact was, he had drunk the water and others had not. That alone may have come to haunt him in retrospect. Daniele's discovery had made it certain. There would be no secrets, no guilty pleasures; the word was out.

Hindsight can be perilous. It not only smoothes out the past with designs and wishes, as it did for many of the oppressors, looking backward over the ugly terrain of their pasts; it can cut like a knife into the heart of one's existence, revealing painful truths that one could not or would not see earlier on. In Levi's own eyes, he and Alberto had gotten caught up in the moment; and even though, rationally speaking, there might have been good reason for doing so—after all, had that water been shared with the entire squad, it may not have satisfied any of them— there was no evading the horror of hindsight. While it can be a balm to soothe one's wounds, it can also create wounds, of the sort that do not readily heal.

A further aspect of Levi's shame had to do with the simple but terrible fact that he had lived and others had not. "Are you ashamed because you are alive in place of another? And in particular, of a man more generous, more sensitive, more useful, wiser, worthier of living than you? You cannot block out such feelings (p. 81). . . . I felt innocent, yes, but enrolled among the saved and therefore in permanent search of a justification in my own eyes and those of others. The worst survived, that is, the fittest; the best all died" (p. 82). So it is, Levi believes, that "we, the survivors, are not the true witnesses" (p. 83). The mere fact that there is any story to tell at all says as much.

Levi addresses one additional dimension of shame toward the end of his essay. In an important sense, it too is about the profound and tragic limits of the present. Levi calls it "the shame of the world." As he explains, "there are those who, faced by the crimes of others or their own, turn their backs so as not to see it and not feel touched by it." Perhaps in virtue of the coercive spell that had been cast upon them, this is what happened to many Germans during Hitler's reign, "deluding themselves that not seeing was a way of not knowing, and that not knowing relieved them of their share of complicity or connivance" (pp. 85–86). There *was* no distance for them, no view from the outside. In a sense, they had sought to will away, through a kind of self-inflicted blindness, consciousness itself, such that they could avoid saying, "Look at what we are doing." As we have seen, for many, the spell lasted beyond the Hitler years, into the future. They could not even say, "Look at what we have *done.*" They did tell stories, but they were stories that had congealed into mythical tales in which the past had been "re-elaborated," as Levi puts it, to suit their own needs and perhaps to defend themselves against some of their own shame.

But Levi and his fellow prisoners had been denied "the screen of willed ignorance":

> The ocean of pain, past and present, surrounded us, and its level rose from year to year until it almost submerged us. It was useless to close one's eyes or turn one's back to it because it was all around, in every direction, all the way to the horizon. It was not possible for us nor did we want to become islands; the just among us, neither more nor less numerous than in any other human group, felt remorse, shame, and pain for the misdeeds that others and not they had committed, and in which they felt involved, because they sensed that what had happened around them and in their presence, and in them, was irrevocable. Never again could it be cleansed; it would prove that man, the human species—we, in short—had the potential to construct an infinite enormity of pain, and that pain is the only force created from nothing, without cost and without effort. It is enough to not see, not to listen, not to act. (p. 86)

The moral dimension looms large in this passage and cuts deep. Ironically, again, it was frequently left to the victims and not the oppressors to look back upon the past and to say, "Look at what we have done"—the "we" here referring not to the victims alone but to the whole of the species.

Alongside what Levi refers to as the shame of the world, we might refer to *the shame of being*. On one level, this shame has to do with the fallen condition of humanity. But it also has to do, I suggest, with our very existence as temporal beings. We are beings who tend to be caught up in the present, blinded by its apparent light, lured by the very proximity of things. The tragic result, I have suggested, is that we are often *late, too* late, in seeing, in realizing, in understanding. Surely a measure of virtue exists in much of what Levi has had to say; the depth of his shame is itself an index of the depth of his conscience and moral commitments. But it is a virtue *deferred,* one that oftentimes must await the awful wisdom of hindsight to become manifest. *"I ought to have done otherwise." "If only I had known." "How could I not see?"*

It should be noted that in the case of Levi's water incident there might have been no story to tell at all had he not been observed by Daniele. There may have been a measure of remorse or regret for having been reduced to such animalistic greed but little more; another event would more than likely have come along and blotted out the first or transformed it into "just another" pitiful display of his and his comrades' sorry state. In a certain sense, the water incident, at the time of its occurrence, was a not-yet-episode—or, if it is preferred, an unspecifiable episode in a yet-to-be-determined narrative. Once Daniele entered the scene, however, an immediate retroactive refiguring of the event occurred: the water was taken away from the likes of *him,* my fellow human, my would-be brother. Bearing this in mind, it seems plausible to say that it is precisely *narrative time* that renders the human condition as precarious, vulnerable, and fragile as it is: we do not know, and cannot know, where the story in which we are engaged will lead.[4] The result is that there is a perpetual slippage, an existential gap, between immediate experience and its retrospective transformation through narrative. The present, despite its presence, is characterized by a kind of absence, as described in Chapter 2.[5] There is something

---

[4] The classic statement on narrative time is provided by Ricoeur, 1981b; see also Ricoeur, 1985, 1988; in relation to self, see Brockmeier, 2000; Freeman, 1998.
[5] See also Lloyd, 1993; Freeman, 2002c.

missing now, in my immediate experience. This something is that future which, in due time, will come along and allow me to see what it is that seems to have gone on. The water is now gone; I am too late. This condition of lateness bespeaks our finitude. We are beings-in-waiting, living uncertainly in the open time of the present, whose absence remains to be filled by the future, which will render it past.

An important qualification must be made here. I do not mean to suggest that the retrospective transformation through narrative is the "last word." Daniele had apparently been a good and decent man. For this reason, Levi's tragic story would likely have remained intact for years to come, colored this way or that by the given telling and its circumstances, but fundamentally unchanged. It is also possible, however, that something might have been learned about Daniele—about his collaboration with the enemy, for instance, or his own greed or weakness or cowardice—that could have changed the story entirely. It was good that they had drunk all that water, Levi might eventually have said; that scoundrel didn't deserve a blessed drop. I offer this hypothetical scenario simply by way of indicating that stories we tell are always provisional and revisable, partly owing to the nature of interpretation and partly owing to the nature of narrative and narrative time: even when I least expect it, a new experience or piece of information may come along that will utterly and completely transform my understanding of the past and the story I tell about it. The finitude that is part and parcel of my being a being-in-waiting is thus magnified, redoubled, by the finitude of my narrative gaze. We might therefore speak of a double deferral or *postponement* that is characteristic of human temporality.

This qualification notwithstanding, let me develop this notion of the narrative gaze by returning to Georges Gusdorf's

(1980) metaphor of the aerial view that I introduced in Chapter 1 and mentioned again earlier in this chapter. From one angle, the sharp contours of reality recede from view as one moves farther and farther away from the ground. Memory, following this metaphor, becomes more schematic, conventional, generic; the fleshy immediacy of the present is replaced by the blurriness of the past. But that is not all that happens when one is given an aerial view of things. As Gusdorf has suggested, just as an aerial view sometimes reveals aspects of a landscape or cityscape invisible to someone on the ground, memory "gives me a certain remove and allows me to take into consideration all the ins and outs of the matter, its context in space and time" (p. 38). What memory also gives me is a sense of the narrative order; for the "remove" about which Gusdorf speaks, far from merely being an empty stretch of time, has been comprised of other experiences, now to be seen in their interrelatedness as episodes in an evolving narrative.

This view from afar can at times be exhilarating; there can be the thrill of insight, of seeing how everything fits together. As Levi well knew, however, this view could also bring about shame and sorrow, precisely in virtue of allowing one to see what could not be seen before. Whether the aerial view of hindsight leads to exhilaration or shame, a certain humility is entailed in realizing both the limited vision that characterizes the present of experience and the consequent possibility of our lateness.

OUR SITUATION

Multiple forms of being-late are possible. Perhaps most severely, there are those situations referred to earlier when one *does* have an idea of the right thing to do and, for whatever reason (weakness, obedience to authority, conformity), doesn't do it.

Despite Levi's own indecision about his culpability, it could be argued that his behavior in the water pipe incident fits this category. The very fact that he knew he had choices and that some of them were more worthy than others is key. Quite different kinds of examples emerge in this context as well. Oftentimes the way we behave with people, particularly those we love, is decidedly less than ideal. We may even acknowledge this during the course of immediate experience as there surfaces a fleeting intimation of our defensiveness or egocentricity or meanness. But there need not even be such an intimation. There are times when we can feel completely justified about carrying on as we do—I am right; you are wrong—only to realize shortly thereafter the fact of our duplicity. Humility may be but a step away from humiliation. I was wrong; an apology is in order.

Less severely, although no less problematically, situations occur in which we can come to realize our own state of oblivion or blindness. Someone had been suffering but we hadn't quite noticed. Or, we say goodbye to someone we hadn't really "seen" for some time only to realize her deep virtues. "Absence makes the heart grow fonder." It can also lead to shame: I ought to have been able to see those virtues all the while. I *could* have seen them. But I did not. It is precisely this sort of situation that leads one to chide oneself. The denial of water and the denial of love are not unrelated.

Other kinds of situations occur in which one should have known, or should have known better. I ought to have done the laundry myself. I ought to have acted more adult-like in that traffic jam with my daughter in the car. I ought to have realized that those words would hurt her. And so on. My aim here is not to catalogue those many circumstances that make us feel guilty or ashamed. Rather, it is to call further attention to the slippage that exists between immediate and remembered experience. Consider the wide variety of emotions that are relevant here. In addition to guilt and shame, there is remorse, regret, embarrassment, not to mention the sheer despairing nausea that sometimes befalls us when it becomes radiantly clear that, in some fundamental way, we have not lived well.

There are also situations in which one couldn't have known (and shouldn't have known), but that still retain a deep and lasting emotional impact. Consider Freud's (1966 [1895]) notion of "deferred action" (*Nachtraglichkeit*), which refers to the idea that, although one may undergo experiences that are not traumatic at the time, they may become so at some later point, as further development makes possible a new understanding of what had occurred. Experiences thus come to acquire new meanings and emotional force by virtue of the distance conferred by time: A strange physical encounter can thus become rewritten as a seduction, a terribly wrong seduction, that will henceforth echo throughout a person's life. Upon seeing this process of deferred action at work, Freud discovered at least two highly significant features of memory. First, he discovered that there seemed to exist memorial "traces," buried, as it were, in some region of the mind inaccessible to consciousness. Second, he discovered that, although the presence of these traces was unquestionably of critical importance in its own right—since it attested to the idea that the past, rather than being wholly superseded by the present and the future, was *preserved* in some fashion—what was even more important was the fact of how the meanings "attached" to these traces *changed* over the course of time. Although Freud had some difficulty fully reconciling this fact in his work, he had thus helped to show that the human past, rather than being some static "thing," was itself a kind of text, progressively rewritten in the light of ongoing experience. Moreover, and again, a human life cannot be understood in linear terms, as a mere chain of discrete causes and effects. Instead, it consists of repetitions and returns, the past being transformed, to a greater or lesser extent, every step of the way by the movement of experience.[6]

Traumas aside, there are experiences about which we have no control whatsoever that nevertheless prove to be pivotal in our own self-formation—or deformation—owing to their being transmuted into the stuff of story. These too may be said to entail a certain humility and bespeak the "alterity"—the deep otherness—of our condition: there is much in our experience that we plainly cannot know until later on—and even then, only provisionally. Perhaps it is realizations of this sort that allow us to see, in addition, that there is much in our experience that we will *never* know. Deferral can be endless.

Finally, there is a form of being-late that has to do with the brute power of fate. I decide to take a short-cut home but get stuck in a traffic jam because of an accident. I go to a party and across the room is the woman who will be my wife. I take a ride home from college with my father and we talk, for the first time in years, and in the wake of his death a month later the ride reverberates through time, becoming a kind of mythical monument. The accidental nature of things, coupled with their often-profound significance in the stories of our lives, gives one pause. What will happen next? What will it mean? And what will it mean later, and later, and later? Fate and finitude: things could have been otherwise. It should be reiterated that the situation I am describing is itself to be located within the fabric of culture and history. As Eliade (1954) reminded us (see Chapter 1), the

---

[6] See Brockmeier, 1997; Freeman, 1985; Lear, 1998; Lukacher, 1986.

phenomenology of time consciousness in "archaic" societies was markedly different from that which characterizes modern societies. The present, such as it was, was imbued with meaning and significance, which had been in existence forever; to live was to participate in those recurrent patterns and timeless stories without which there could *be* no reality. Things could *not* have been otherwise in the era of mythical time but only what they were, then as always. With the movement toward historical time, with its endless series of moments, marching on, one after the other, all of this changed, radically: the present would become an open, indeterminate space, largely devoid of meaning—or at least stable and enduring meaning of the sort that had once been available. As such, it would henceforth have to await hindsight for its meaning to be discerned, with the narrative imagination assuming center stage. Narrative reflection in modernity, therefore, becomes a vehicle of recollection and recuperation, a vestige of the mythopoeic realm, surpassed and yet alive, still. Hence the situation in which we find ourselves: living in waiting, in anticipation, not quite knowing what is going on now, much less what the future will bring, and relying on hindsight, again and again, to discern what meaning there may be.

FAITH AND FUTURITY

This situation may be magnified in those of us who are living our lives without the anchor of religion. Levi himself was not a believer. He does note that believers generally "lived better" throughout their ordeal in the camps. He speaks of "the saving force of their faith," and suggests that, "Their universe was vaster than ours, more extended in space and time, above all more comprehensible: they had a key and a point of leverage, a millennial tomorrow so that there might be a sense to sacrificing themselves, a place in heaven or on earth where justice and compassion had won, or would win in a perhaps remote but certain future" (p. 146). Levi was denied all of this meaning and solace, this *hope*. What he was not denied—indeed, what he *could* not deny—was the conviction of his having participated, in some way, in the very crimes that had been perpetrated against him. More than shame was at work. Shame is something one might be able to work through and beyond; it is a malady of the self, and lends itself to some measure of change. What Levi had experienced, I suggest, might more appropriately be considered *sin*. It was a malady of the soul, and it could not become an object of change, of reconstruction. Hence the depth of the tragedy: here is what one might plausibly call religious experience, in a radically negative form, but with no religious resources available to allow for the possibility of atonement or redemption. The damage is done. It's too late.

It should be reiterated that there is a much more positive side to this situation, to be explored further in the final chapter of this book. The very fact of Levi's having to struggle with his own sense of sin, after the fact, may itself be understood as testimony to his own sense of the sacred, the Good. To recognize the depravity of the species, and to suffer from this recognition as much as he did, are themselves signs of virtue. On some level, they are indeed signs of *transcendence*, of a going-beyond both the confines of the present and the evil that sometimes accompanies it. For Levi to tell this tragic story, in other words, he himself had to have known that there was a better way. The recognition of his, and humanity's, potential sinfulness is inseparable from the revelation of the soul's depth. If only he could have received some consolation from this simple fact.

Let me offer three ideas in closing. As has been suggested, there is a dimension of lateness intrinsic to the movement of self-understanding: insight frequently arrives late on the scene, after one has gathered enough distance from past experience to discern its meaning and significance. Tolstoy's story of Ivan Ilych (1960 [1886]) provides a classic example of exactly this: faced with the reality of his imminent death, Ilych looks back upon his life only to find wreckage. Fortunately for him, he does ultimately manage to let in a bit of light. And in that sense, one might argue, it is never *entirely* too late to begin to repair the brokenness of the soul. There remains room for a kind of recollective "rescue effort" through narrative, through reimagining and refashioning the past. But this idea of lateness—the after-the-fact nature of so much of moral life, in particular—nevertheless remains a central feature of the human condition. Virtue is frequently postponed, deferred.

Perhaps more important for present purposes than this notion of deferral, however, is the horizon of meaning, perhaps even of *ultimate* meaning, that often seems to provide the backdrop to the process of remembering the past. What is it that leads Primo Levi to look back on his own awful experience in the camps only to find there his own culpability and complicity? "Are you ashamed," he had asked, "because you are alive in place of another? And in particular, of a man more generous, more sensitive, more useful, wiser, worthier of living than you?" (1989, p. 81). Here, we might ask: Where do such feelings come from? And how do they come to acquire the power, and permanence, they do? The same sorts of questions might be posed in conjunction with those who, on looking backward on the landscape of their lives, experience great joy and gratitude. There are, of course, many answers one might give to these sorts of questions, some of them quite unmysterious. One feels badly for having fallen sorely short of widely held societal expectations. Or one feels good for having met, or exceeded, such expectations.

The issues here, in other words, might have to do with little more than social self-esteem.

In hearing a story like Primo Levi's, however, this kind of account seems inadequate. His perceived failure cuts deep, and the kinds of images he has of who might have been "worthier of living" than he was seem to go beyond social ideals. "In lyric poetry," in contrast to the novel, Helen Vendler (1995) writes,

> voice is made abstract. It may tell you one specific thing about itself—that it is black, or that it is old, or that it is female, or that it is celibate. But it will not usually tell you, if it is black, that it grew up in Atlanta rather than Boston; or, if it is old, how old it is; or, if it is female, whether it is married; or, if it is celibate, when it took its vows. . . . The range of things one would normally know about a voice in a novel one does not know about a voice in a lyric. What one does know, if it is socially specified at all, is severely circumscribed. (p. 3)

As Vendler goes on to suggest, "If the normal home of selfhood is the novel, which ideally allows many aspects of the self, under several forms, to expatiate and take on substance, then the normal home of 'soul' is the lyric, where the human being becomes a set of warring passions independent of time and space" (p. 5).

One may of course argue that, strictly speaking, no such passions exist wholly "independent of time and space." Passions are themselves historically situated and, on some level, socially constructed. Following Vendler, however, it may be that there exist dimensions of the inner life that exceed this more local situatedness. She thus speaks of those times when "the self is alone with itself, when its socially constructed characteristics . . . are felt to be in abeyance" (p. 7). If Vendler is right about this— that is, if she is right in making this distinction between self and soul, each of which represents a vitally important aspect of the human person—it follows that the life story may embody both of these aspects. In part, it will be about particulars, tied to the changing circumstances of one's life. But in addition, the story one tells may also be about fundamental, even ultimate, questions, tied to enduring features of the human condition. One might therefore speak, cautiously, of the *transcendent horizon* of the life story, by which I refer to those dimensions of the life story that are, finally, about the state and destiny of one's very soul. Why transcendent? The reason is that the operative terms in a case such as Levi's—for instance, worthiness, justification—appear to refer to ideals that transcend societal norms and expectations and point toward images of fulfillment and completion that are difficult to contain within a purely immanent framework. Indeed, they refer to images that are difficult to "contain" at all. Plato's "form of the Good" comes to mind here: never encountered face to face in the earthly world, it nonetheless provides a horizon of ultimate meaning and value that conditions the very judgments that can be made about right and wrong, good and bad.

The final idea has to do with the deep shame that Levi had experienced—which, I suggested, might better be regarded as sin—and what might be done about it. Here, I will simply suggest that crises of memory, such as his, can only be met with faith, such that some measure of absolution can be brought about. For some, this faith will be explicitly religious in nature. Forgiveness—*self*-forgiveness—will likely be a key feature. For others, however—such as Levi—it will have to do with reconciling themselves not only to the personal past but to the human condition itself, and the moral lateness that often characterizes it. If Levi's story is any indication, this challenge is a massive and vitally important one, having to do with nothing less than the remaking of the soul. Only then will it be possible to move into the future and keep one's story alive.

FOUR

THE NARRATIVE UNCONSCIOUS

"MEMORY"

I can picture Primo Levi, vaguely, as he drinks water from that pipe during that hot August day in Auschwitz. I can also see his friend Alberto nearby, looking furtively to make sure no one sees, and Daniele, parched and ashen, his look of bitter resentment upon discovering the two. Needless to say, I have never actually seen any of these people; I have simply read a book, with characters and scenes vivid enough to come to life. These characters and scenes have become part of my imagination, part of the gallery of images that I can draw upon as I try to make sense of things. In a distinct and important sense, they are part of my *memory* as well—not, of course, my memory of characters and scenes I have witnessed firsthand but memory nonetheless, peopled with images of things past that are every bit as real as those deriving from firsthand experience. Indeed, I would go so far as to say that the images I have of Levi and Alberto and Daniele and countless others I have "met" only indirectly are part of my *history,* of the stream of experiences that have come my way during the course of my life. This, however, brings us to a paradox of sorts. Not only have I never encountered Levi and company directly, but the scenes I bring to mind took place before I was even born. At the same time, I have suggested that these very scenes are themselves part of my memory and history. It might be added that they bear upon my *identity* as well. How can this be?

Thus far, I have been dealing with the issue of hindsight exclusively in the context of individuals' lives, that is, in the span of time that stretches between birth and death. Working from this perspective, narrative reflection may be seen as an effort to give form and meaning to the trajectory of events, experiences, and epochs that emerge in and through hindsight. These events, experiences, and epochs are generally assumed to be *mine*—affected, no doubt, by external factors, but separable from them. We shall have reason to question this assumption in the pages to come. What's more, we shall have reason to question the further assumption that "my story" is restricted to the span of time between my birth and death. For, insofar as memory is itself an amalgam of both first- and secondhand sources, sources that may in fact lie beyond the borders of an individual life, the scope of narrative understanding expands vastly.

In this chapter, I explore the process by which sources beyond the perimeter of the individual become woven into the fabric of memory, resulting in what I call the "narrative unconscious." With this phrase, I refer not to that more private, secretive dimension of the unconscious posited by psychoanalysis but to the cultural dimension—specifically, to those culturally rooted aspects of one's history that remain uncharted and that, consequently, have yet to be incorporated into one's story. An important challenge thus arises for those fashioning autobiographical narratives, whether explicitly in writing or implicitly in reflection: insofar as the narrative unconscious is operative in one's history, there exists the need to move *beyond* personal life in telling one's own story, into the shared life of culture.

I begin by turning once more to an experience from my own life that has come to inform my thinking about these issues.[1] Back in 1997, I had the opportunity to visit Berlin for the first time. From the very start, I found it to be an extraordinarily interesting city, by virtue of its music and art and architecture, its colorful street culture, and, of course, its history. It was quite unlike any other city I had ever visited. But I found myself unprepared for a couple of things that came to characterize my stay. The first was what seemed to be a ceaseless, and painfully difficult, process of collective reflection on the crimes of the past, both in the media and in everyday talk. This was not the only thing people talked about; plenty of other issues were in the air at the time. But it was striking just how ubiquitous this set of concerns seemed to be in the minds and hearts of many of the people of Berlin. The moral dimension of hindsight is painfully evident in this context: to think that so many people had imagined, not too long ago, that what they were doing was not only acceptable but *good*. Never before that visit had I had such an acute sense of an entire social body, or at least a significant portion of it, being engaged in recollective—and reconstructive—work. It was, and remains, much-needed.

The second thing that characterized my stay in Berlin is more personal. Although I approached visiting Berlin with some measure of uncertainty over how I would respond to being there—given my own Jewish background, the books I had

---

[1] See Freeman, 2001, 2002a.

read, the movies I had seen, and so on—I didn't experience any particular intensity about the prospect. For one, the first few days were to be spent at an academic conference, where the topics had little to do with Germany and its past. For another, I would be with friends who lived in Berlin and were eager to show me around, share some food and drink, and have a good time. As it turned out, the conference was in fact uneventful, as were the first couple of days touring the city. We saw lots of sights, we shared some meals, and, in the face of all the cranes dotting the landscape, we talked a good deal about the challenges the city faced as it sought to rebuild itself, literally and figuratively. It was all fascinating to me, but in a somewhat distanced way. There were emotions, to be sure, but they were blunted and rather generic: "How terrible it must have been." "It's all so hard to imagine." "It's incredible how fresh the wounds still seem to be, all those buildings, pieces ripped out of them by shells, the commemorative plaques, the armed guards in front of synagogues, even now." And so forth and so on.

But then something strange, and utterly unexpected, happened. I still don't know quite how to make sense of it. I was traveling on a bus through the city when everything that had been at a distance suddenly came near: the cranes, the buildings, the gardens, the Brandenburg Gate, the Reichstag. Everything that had been a fascinating or disturbing spectacle, an object to be beheld, taken in—as when one takes in the sights of any city—had become a kind of living, breathing presence. When I initially tried to explain this to someone, I said that I had never had such an intense experience of *history* as I had had then, during those moments.

As for my response to this sudden transformation from spectacle to presence, it was something like a deep grief, a mixture of sorrow and horror, rolled into one. I was either weeping or on the verge of it for a good amount of time afterward. It was very strange and very powerful. Generally speaking, I am not given to this sort of emotional outburst, but there was something truly extraordinary about this experience, and I found it extremely disturbing.

What had happened? My first impulse led me down an almost mystical path. As I said to someone later in the day, after the storm had passed, it was as if death was in the air, and everything else—the buildings, the gardens, and so on—saturated in it. Phenomenologically, in other words, everything that I suddenly found menacing or sorrowful was wholly *Other,* wholly outside of me. Odd though it was to consider, I couldn't help but wonder whether it was possible for the events of the past—terrible ones, in particular—to somehow leave traces, in the form of disturbed energy fields or some such thing. I am not talking here about material traces, concrete reminders of events past, which were of course everywhere, but nonmaterial ones. Recall some of those fabled stories where family after family moves into their beautiful new suburban home only to find that there's something in one of the rooms—a creaking noise, the sound of a crying child, a muffled scream—that keeps them awake at night. They also talk about how strange the room is, how different it is from all the others. At some point they race off to the local library and scan through old newspapers only to find that a violent crime had taken place there, years ago. . . . Without going quite this far, I did in fact find myself entertaining the idea that the past could somehow become inscribed in the present, that in some fundamental way it remained alive and operative. Would someone who stumbled upon a piece of land where a concentration camp once stood, without knowing where he or she was, feel anything different? Would there be traces or echoes, even *ghosts* of a sort? It is possible. But the modern mind—including my own—finds it difficult to move into regions like these, intriguing though they are.

A less mystical version of all this might simply speak of *absence*—or, as discussed in Chapter 2, the presence of what is missing. Whatever was *there* existed in relation to what was not. As I scrawled down later in some notes, it was as if a great hole existed in the middle of history. A part of us was missing from humanity. And a part of humanity was missing from us.

But then I had to pull back a bit. Somehow or other, I had to presume, I must have "brought" ideas with me that set in motion the experiences of the day. That is to say, I must have been hermeneutically "prepared" in some way to experience all those things in the way I did. But how? What exactly was it that I had brought there?

As the philosopher George Allan (1993) has pointed out, the understandings and practices we employ as we navigate through the world are in part "implicit and unthematized, habits of the heart or mind or muscles" (p. 24) that are to be considered nonconscious elements of *tradition.* "The most fundamental of these habits," he continues, "these unreflective ways of taking things and interacting with them, constitute my cultural horizon" (p. 24).[2] As Allan goes on to suggest, "we make ourselves by how we use what is provided for us. . . . Individual selves," in other words, are made "by giving concrete shape to possibilities made available by their traditions within the exigencies of present experience" (p. 37). This nonconscious dimension of tradition as applied to self,

---

[2] See also Gadamer, 1975; Jauss, 1989.

therefore, has to do with the personal imprint or signature that is fashioned out of the givens of culture. I brought a *world* to that trip to Berlin, a cultural horizon, which surely contributed to the experiences of the day.

Second, I likely brought a good deal of *knowledge* from books and movies, photographs, and any number of other such things. I am not especially knowledgeable about Berlin; it's not as if I had a working road map in my mind that would allow me to say, "Oh, this is where this happened, that is where that happened." But presumably, I had carried with me a significant enough store of common knowledge and common imagery as to activate the undercurrents of some of the things I witnessed. "Memory," in this context, becomes a curious amalgam of fact and fiction, experiences and texts, documentary footage, dramatizations, movies, plays, television shows, fantasies, and more.

Third, there is little doubt but that my Jewish background entered the picture as well—although quite honestly, it is difficult to say exactly how. I am not a deeply religious person. Nor do I have much direct knowledge of family members who suffered at the hands of the Nazis. So it's not as if I brought along a well-articulated set of anticipations and expectations about what I would find. Nevertheless, it was evident that my own religious and cultural identity as a Jew had played a significant role in how I had responded to the scenes I had encountered. The following morning, in fact, I went on a kind of pilgrimage to a synagogue in the city. It didn't have to be a specific synagogue, and it didn't have be the site of some horrific crime. It simply had to be a synagogue, a place where "my people" had been. In speaking of "my people," I do so with full acknowledgment—which isn't to say full understanding—of the complexities involved. The fact is, I hadn't been all that connected, at least not directly, to "my people," the Jewish people. And so, as I reflect back on the experience and try to make sense of it, I need to figure this fact into the equation. Why, given my own ambivalences and uncertainties and hesitations, had there been such a powerful encounter? Was it *despite* all these things? Was it *because* of them? Was it due to there being an admixture of identification and nonidentification, approach and avoidance, connection and disconnection? I do not know. One thing, however, had become clear. And that was that there existed dimensions of my own history—or, put somewhat differently, dimensions of history that had somehow figured into the constellation I call "my life"—about which I had been largely unaware. I could see this in hindsight.

In some ways, the connection I am positing here—between the experience in Berlin and the underground history that seems to have led to it—is reminiscent of the connection I had considered back in Chapter 2, between my intense fear in the face of my daughter's pneumonia and my father's sudden death years before. Much the same temporal dynamic is at work as well. I have just used the language of "led to," which implies that my heretofore unacknowledged history had somehow caused or provoked the experience in Berlin. This does seem plausible on some level. But of course it wasn't until I actually *had* that experience that this would-be cause—which would never have risen to this status otherwise—emerged. Levi's encounter with Daniele is relevant here too: only upon that dreadful encounter would those secret gulps of water come to instigate the shame that had ensued. As Ned Lukacher (1986) has noted in his reflections on the interconnections between literature, philosophy, and psychoanalysis, at work here is "a double or 'metaleptic' logic in which causes are both the causes of effects and the effects of effects" (p. 35).[3] Such is the nature of narrative reason. In the present case, however, a difference exists as well—namely, that the provoking cause I have posited for my Berlin experience, a cause I have been considering under the rubric of "memory," is comprised of realities, operating unconsciously, that are largely secondhand, outside the perimeter of direct experience.

But am I really talking about "memory"? Is that the appropriate term to use here? Consider what Susan Sontag has to say about photographs in *Regarding the Pain of Others* (2003):

> The familiarity of certain photographs builds our sense of the present and immediate past. Photographs lay down routes of reference, and serve as totems of causes: sentiment is more likely to crystallize around a photograph than around a verbal slogan. And photographs help construct—and revise—our sense of a more distant past, with the posthumous shocks engineered by the circulation of hitherto unknown photographs. Photographs that everyone recognizes are now part of what society chooses to think about, or declares that it has chosen to think about. It calls these ideas "memories," and that is, over the long run, a fiction. Strictly speaking, there is no such thing as collective memory. (p. 85)

"All memory," Sontag goes on to argue, "is individual, unreproducible—it dies with each person." What is often referred to as "collective memory," therefore,

---

[3] Nietzsche's (1968 [1888]) comments about "the phenomenalism of the inner world" are relevant here once again as are Freud's (1962 [1896]; 1966 [1895]) comments about "deferred action." See also Brooks, 1985; Nehamas, 1985; Ricoeur, 1981b.

is not a remembering but a stipulating: that this is important, and this is the story about how it happened, with the pictures that lock the stories in our minds. Ideologies create substantiating archives of images, representative images, which encapsulate common ideas of significance and trigger predictable thoughts, feelings. Poster-ready photographs—the mushroom cloud of an A-bomb test, Martin Luther King, Jr., speaking at the Lincoln Memorial in Washington, D.C., the astronaut walking on the moon—are the visual equivalent of sound bites. They commemorate, in no less blunt fashion than postage stamps, Important Historical Moments; indeed, the triumphalist ones (the picture of the A-bomb excepted) become postage stamps. Fortunately, there is no signature picture of the Nazi death camps. (p. 86)

It is true; there is no such "signature picture." But it is no less true that images of exactly those camps, with their skeleton bodies heaped atop one another, in deep pits, while those on the rim of the abyss do what's needed to erase them from the world, circulate widely in and through the modern mind. Images of just this sort, derived from multiple sources and supplemented by the imagination, had no doubt been operative in some way during that strange episode in Berlin. And they are surely operative in the memories we have of events and experiences that take place during our own lifetime. This in turn suggests that "personal" memory is also, to a greater or lesser extent, a "stipulating," as Sontag puts it: "that this is important, and this is the story about how it happened, with the pictures that lock the stories in our minds."

Whether to use the term "memory" in this context remains an open question, to be explored later in this chapter. For now, I simply wish to underscore the profound ways in which the cultural-historical world becomes inscribed, often unknowingly, in the inner recesses of the mind and the self. This suggests that there are in fact unconscious elements at work, having to do with those largely unrecognized and in turn uncognized aspects of our own histories that are operative in our ongoing engagement with the world. Hence, the idea of the narrative unconscious, which we become aware of precisely during those moments when, through hindsight, our own historical and cultural situatedness comes into view. Hence, in addition, the idea that alongside the manifest narrative of one's life there exists a kind of *counter*-narrative, one that supplements— and perhaps undermines—those ordinary understandings that constitute our "working view" of self.[4] Along these lines, explicating the narrative unconscious vastly expands not only the scope of narrative reflection but of selfhood itself. For "I" am the terminus not only of my own unique history but also of the history that precedes me and that surpasses my own borders.

FIRST- AND SECOND-ORDER MEMORY

Rather than pursuing the vagaries of my own autobiography any further, let me turn to a work that does particularly well in fleshing out the issues at hand. In the introductory pages of Eva Hoffman's book, *After Such Knowledge: Memory, History, and the Legacy of the Holocaust* (2004), she writes:

> I had grown up with a consciousness of the Shoah from the beginning. My parents had emerged from its crucible shortly before my birth. They had survived, in what was then the Polish

---

[4] See especially Bamberg and Andrews' (2004) edited volume *Considering Counter-Narratives: Narrating, Resisting, Making Sense.*

part of the Ukraine, with the help of Polish and Ukrainian neighbors; but their entire families perished. Those were the inescapable facts—the inescapable knowledge—I had come into. But the knowledge had not always been equally active, nor did I always want to make the inheritance defining.

Indeed, it was not until I started writing about it in my first book . . . that I began discerning, amidst other threads, the Holocaust strand of my history. I had carried this part of my psychic past within me all my life; but it was only now, as I began pondering it from a longer distance and through the clarifying process of writing, that what had been an inchoate, obscure knowledge appeared to me as a powerful theme and influence in my life. Until then, it had not occurred to me that I was in effect a receptacle of a historical legacy, or that its burden had a significance and weight that needed to be acknowledged. Now, personal memory appeared to me clearly linked to a larger history, and the heavy dimensions of this inheritance started becoming fully apparent. (p. x)

Hoffman had discovered what I have been calling the narrative unconscious. For her, this discovery had a particular intensity by virtue of her membership in "the second generation," which she refers to as "the hinge generation in which received, transferred knowledge of events is transmuted into history, or into myth" (p. xv).

Hoffman immediately goes on to acknowledge that, "while it has become routine to speak of the 'memory' of the Holocaust, and to adduce to this faculty a moral, even a spiritual value, . . . we who came after do not have memories of the Holocaust. Even from my most intimate proximity," she writes, "I could not form 'memories' of the Shoah or take my parents' memories as my own. Rather, I took in that first information as a sort of fairy tale deriving not so much from another world as from the center of the cosmos: an enigmatic but real fable" (p. 6). And yet, there is a distinct sense in which her parents' memories *did* become her own, albeit of a different order:

> In my childish mind, the hypervivid moments summoned by my parents registered themselves as half awful reality, half wondrous fairy tale. A peasant's hut, holding the riddle of life or death; a snowy forest, which confounds the senses and sense of direction. A hayloft in which one sits, awaiting fate, while a stranger downstairs, who is really a good fairy in disguise, is fending off that fate by muttering invocations under her breath and bringing to the hiding place a bowl of soup. The sister, young, innocent, and loved, standing naked above a pit that is soon to become her own mass grave . . . . The pursuit of powerless people, bent silhouettes running desperately through an exposed landscape, trying to make it into the bordering woods . . . . Fields, trenches, pits of death. For others, barbed wire, skeletal figures, smoke, intimations of mass death. Every survivor's child has such images available right behind the eyelids. Later, through literature and film, through memoirs and oral testimony, these components of horror become part of a whole generation's store of imagery and narration, the icons and sagas of the post-Holocaust world. (pp. 11–12)

Images aside, Hoffman had "absorbed [her] parents' unhappiness through channels that seemed nearly physical. The pain of their psyches," she writes, "reverberated in my body almost as if they were mine" (p. 14).

It is difficult to know how far to take this line of thinking. Hoffman herself is uneasy about the matter. As she explains,

"It was not that the mythical vision of the world I had put together from scraps of story and imagery was untrue. The mythology, after all, derived from reality. It was just that I knew it *as* mythology and had no way of grasping its actuality" (p. 16). Two points deserve emphasis here. The first is that the "mythology" of which Hoffman speaks is not wholly to be severed from memory: this world she has put together, that has become *her* world, is rooted in her own bodily and psychical experiences; these too are "events," although of a different sort than those experienced by her parents. The second point is that memory, whether first- or second-order, is not wholly to be severed from mythology, from those "scraps of story and imagery" that often find their way into the figuration of actuality.

Hoffman goes on to speak of much larger events, having to do with Poland, the Warsaw uprising, and so on, events that were far more distant than those that came to her by way of her parents. These too, she writes, "would become my meaningful history, the history it is urgent to know because it belongs to one's life, because it shapes ancestral fate and one's own sensibility" (p. 18). Such are "the paradoxes of indirect knowledge," a knowledge that continues to "haunt" Hoffman and others who "came after":

> The formative events of the twentieth century have crucially informed our biographies and psyches, threatening sometimes to overshadow and overwhelm our lives. But we did not see them, suffer through them, experience their impact directly. Our relationship to them has been defined by our very "postness," and by the powerful but mediated forms of knowledge that have followed from it. (p. 25)

"There are so many ways to conceive of our lives, our identities, our stories," Hoffman adds—"to shape memory and biography. It did not occur to me to think of myself as a 'child of Holocaust survivors' for many of my adult years. Other threads of causality, influence, development seemed more important; or at least I gave them other names. . . . Identities are malleable and multidimensional," she continues, "and I am reluctant to fix my own through reifying labels. And yet, we do not only define ourselves; we are also defined by our circumstances, culture, the perceptions of others and—perhaps most of all—the force of an internalized past" (p. 27).

One could argue here that this new label Hoffman is employing is simply a new lens through which to view her past. That is to say, it could have nothing whatsoever to do with memory, much less the narrative unconscious; there may be little more at work than the importation of a new sociological category to the trajectory of her life. On my reading, however, Hoffman's new way of conceiving of her life has the force of a revelation, a discovery: through hindsight, she has come to see quite new "threads of causality, influence, development," ones that had been operative and yet unacknowledged, unseen. Her identity had been defined and constituted in ways that had been essentially unbeknownst to her, and with her discovery she has radically enlarged the scope of her own history as well as the story she can now tell about it.

The philosopher and sociologist Maurice Halbwachs' (1992) notion of "collective memory" is surely relevant to this discussion.[5] But in line with Hoffman's reluctance to even employ the

---

[5] There is a rich literature on social and cultural memory deriving from a variety of disciplines. See, e.g., Andrews, 2007; Brockmeier, 2002; Fentress & Wickham, 1992; Zerubavel, 2004.

term "memory" in her story, this notion is problematic in its own right, "veering between a useful and a misleading fiction. For within such 'memory,' "—Hoffman continues to place the term "memory" in quotes—"there is no subject who remembers, no process of remembering, no link between reflection and experience" (pp. 165–166). Her perspective is thus reminiscent of Sontag's. More problematic still is the fact that such "impersonal memory, much more than embodied, personal remembering, is malleable in the extreme, and highly susceptible to deliberate shaping or exploitation—to propaganda and censorship, to tendentious selectivity and willful emphasis. It is, in other words, an instrument not so much of subjective reflection or understanding as of cultural agendas or ideological purposes" (p. 166).

Hoffman is surely right about this, at least in part. My own experience in Berlin, as well as the various experiences she relates, removed as they are from the actualities that are their ultimate referents, are the products of highly schematized images of people and places and things. Put another way, they are the product of memorial *forms,* prototypical patterns or templates, inflected with whatever firsthand knowledge as might have been acquired. With first-order autobiographical memory, there is at least an "anchor," so to speak, of actuality, however schematically and conventionally this actuality may be viewed. With second-order autobiographical memory—should we elect to retain the term—the anchor is gone; and in its place is a kind of montage, a poetically figured heterogeneous image, rounded off at the edges, perhaps as much a function of Hollywood as of our own personal experience.

For Hoffman, the notion of "mediation" looms large: "those who have not lived through the Shoah received its knowledge, at this late date, through mediations—sometimes several layers of them" (p. 178). But this is also true, to a greater or lesser degree, for those who *have* lived through the Shoah—or anything else. For them too, memory is suffused with all kinds of "extraneous" matter. Moreover, it is thoroughly conditioned by one's ever-changing vantage point at the present moment of remembering and narrating. Once again, I emphatically do not wish to *equate* the two situations. For epistemological as well as moral reasons, to do so would simply be wrong. Nevertheless, the fact remains that many of the defining characteristics of *second*-order autobiographical memory may also be found in *first*-order autobiographical memory. Ultimately, in fact, one dimension differentiates the two: the aforementioned "anchor," which entails a reference to the existence of what had once been sensorially present.

But the question remains: Are we really talking here about *memory?* In the final pages of her book, Hoffman suggests that she, and other members of the second generation, need "to disentangle the spectral memories that have inhabited us from the realities we inhabit" (p. 278). From this perspective, there seems to be an advantage of sorts to these memories being "spectral" rather than being rooted in external realities. Because these spectral memories are without anchor, perhaps they can dissipate more easily or be separated out from the actual. This line of thinking is in keeping with Hoffman's uncertainty about whether to even call the phenomenon she has been exploring "memory," and she is perfectly right to try to determine the ways in which her own narrative unconscious has been shaped by propaganda, by ideological designs and agendas, all of which have led her to a too stereotypical view of history and of her own past. What we see in her story, however, is that this very project of "disentanglement" of others' memories from one's own, of the actual from the fantastic—which presumes that it is somehow possible to extricate ourselves from history and, in essence, to reconstruct our identity anew and afresh, *without* spectral adornments—cannot be brought to completion. What we also see is that the work of hindsight must go beyond the particularities of "my history," into the larger history in and through which one's life assumes its distinctive form.

HINDSIGHT AND HISTORY

To develop further this connection between "my history" and the larger history to which it belongs, I shall draw briefly on two other exemplary stories. The first is Jill Ker Conway's memoir *The Road from Coorain* (1989), a story that recounts her life growing up in the Australian bush, coming to terms with her own identity as a woman and an Australian, and, eventually, leaving her homeland to carry forward her own projects and plans as an educator. In large measure, Conway's narrative is a traditional one, about her own unique, personal circumstances. In addition, however, it is about her formation as a social being and especially about her own process of coming-to-consciousness about certain elements of this formation that had remained occluded, hidden from view. Upon meeting a teacher who had been "impatient with Australian bourgeois culture," she eventually came to understand that she herself was being formed educationally in such a way as to minimize, even erase, the influences of her own country. Hindsight is thus suffused with humility: "We might have been in Sussex," she writes, "for all the attention we paid to Australian poetry and prose." Conway and her classmates would memorize Keats and Shelley, for instance, their vivid descriptions of nature, which had given them "the impression that great poetry and fiction were written by and about people and places far distant from Australia" (p. 99). What this had also done, Conway recognized, was give them the impression that their own natural world, which deviated greatly from these poetic descriptions, was somehow inferior, second-rate.

As for Australia itself, it had its own share of problems—some of which, Conway had discovered, lay beneath her very feet. Her family had occupied a large expanse of land that she had always taken to be theirs. But "Who," she eventually had to ask, "were the rightful owners and users of the land I had always thought to belong to us?" (p. 170). Among other things, she remembers having stumbled across aboriginal ovens and strange stones, which she herself had "heedlessly trodden upon" throughout much of her life. She hadn't really given these things a thought, having assumed they had merely been abandoned, by choice. Her lack of awareness, which came into view as she gazed backward upon her past, proved to be extremely disturbing. It was as if she had been shaken awake from a deep slumber.

Later on, when despite her qualifications she was rejected for a job because she was a woman, Conway had been shaken awake yet again, her past becoming transformed once more. "I could not credit that merit could not win me a place in an endeavor I wanted to undertake, that decisions about my eligibility were made on the mere fact of my being female instead of on my talents. . . . It was prejudice, blind prejudice" (p. 191). From this point, she writes, "I could never remember the image of my parents resting in the evening, sitting on the front veranda step at Coorain, quite the same again" (p. 191). Conway's narrative had thus been immeasurably complicated by her discoveries. She had been an actor in a history she did not know, or that she knew only partially and incompletely. And when this *history* became part of her *story,* her life itself took on new and more complex dimensions. What Conway had come to articulate through these experiences, therefore, was precisely a series of counter-narratives, which in turn required that she rewrite not only her past but her very self. These counter-narratives, she realized, had to be integrated into her evolving sense of identity; without them, there would only be a superficial and incomplete rendition of the past, one that mistook the manifest order of things for the whole story.

The second book I want to consider is poet Czeslaw Milosz's *Native Realm* (1981), which is subtitled *A Search for Self-Definition*. At the outset of the book, Milosz writes: "I am beginning a quest, a voyage into the heart of my own, yet not only my own, past" (p. 3). Not unlike Hoffman and Conway, he wishes to talk about a past that will not be strictly personal but will instead move beyond the boundaries of his own life and world. "The vision of a small patch on the globe to which I owe everything," he continues, "suggests where I should draw the line. A three-year-old's love for his aunt or jealousy toward his father takes up so much room in autobiographical writings because everything else, for instance the history of a country or a national group, is treated as something 'normal' and, there-fore, of little interest to the narrator. But another method is possible" (p. 5), Milosz suggests:

> Instead of thrusting the individual into the foreground, one can focus attention on the background, looking upon oneself as a sociological phenomenon. Inner experience, as it is preserved in the memory, will then be evaluated in the perspective of the changes one's milieu has undergone. The passing over of certain periods important for oneself, but requiring too personal an explanation, will be a token of respect for those undergrounds that exist in all of us and are better left in peace. (pp. 5–6)

Milosz will therefore attend to different "undergrounds" in his search for self-definition, ones that will allow him to see some of the supra-personal elements that have become woven into the fabric of his memory and his life. I am not sure whether "looking upon oneself as a sociological phenomenon" is the most appropriate way to frame the methodological questions at hand. In fact, I am not sure it is what Milosz's own auto-biographical enterprise is about. His most basic challenge is rather to look at his own personal world in dialogue with the wider world, in order to see how its broad currents had been operative. "The awareness of one's origins," he goes on to note, "is like an anchor plunged into the deep, keeping one within a certain range. Without it, historical intuition is virtually impossible" (p. 20).

As Milosz also notes, "Knowledge does not have to be conscious. It is incredible how much of the aura of a country can penetrate to a child. Stronger than thought is an image—of dry leaves on a path, of twilight, of a heavy sky. In the park, revolutionary patrols whistled back and forth to each other. The Volga was the color of black lead. I carried away forever the impression of concealed terror, of inexpressible dialogues confided in a whisper or a wink of the eye" (p. 45). Just as Milosz speaks about unconscious knowledge, the images and stories of his childhood having become part of the very fabric of his life, so too does he speak about his self and its formation:

In a certain sense I consider myself a typical Eastern European. It seems to be true that his *differentia specifica* can be boiled down to a lack of form—both inner and outer. His good qualities—intellectual avidity, fervor in discussion, a sense of irony, freshness of feeling, spatial (or geographical) fantasy—

derive from a basic weakness: he always remains an adolescent, governed by a sudden ebb or flow of inner chaos. Form is achieved in stable societies. My own case is enough to verify how much of an effort it takes to absorb contradictory traditions, norms, and an overabundance of impressions, and to put them into some kind of order. The things that surround us in childhood need no justification, they are self-evident. If, however, they whirl about like particles in a kaleidoscope, ceaselessly changing position, it takes no small amount of energy simply to plant one's feet on solid ground without falling. (p. 67)

It may be useful to consider an incident Milosz recounts that, in an important sense, is about the workings of the narrative unconscious. It also ties in well, albeit obliquely, with some of what I discussed earlier regarding my own strange encounter with Berlin. He writes:

I have the scene before me now: spring sun shining into our classroom windows, sparrows chirping, the first of May. Our French teacher . . . looks at me suspiciously. He beckons me to him with his finger. I go up to his table, my hair is unkempt, I am twelve years old. "What do you have there?" Sticking out of my pocket are the forks of a slingshot. "What are you going to do with that?" I try to give my voice a hard, masculine ring. "Beat Jews." He narrows his eyes in a cold reflex as if he were looking at an animal. I feel hot, I feel as if had turned beet-red. He confiscates the weapon.

Had I really meant to use the slingshot against Sashka and Sonka [two Jewish children from his neighborhood]? No concrete man was my adversary. I carried within myself an abstraction, a creature without a face, a fusion of concepts bearing a minus sign. What is more, I was aware of it not as my own, not something inborn, but as alien. And during my run-in with the teacher, the shame I felt was made all the more painful by a sudden illumination that revealed the real instigator. It was one of my relatives, whom I despised. I suddenly saw the connection between my attitude and his political harangues at the dinner table, when I seemed not to be but was listening. From that moment on, every nationalist slogan was to remind me of his pitiful person. (p. 96)

Compelling though this story is, it is difficult to know what to make of it. I do not doubt the incident itself; it is of the sort that can get emblazoned in one's memory, standing as a kind of mythical monument, not unlike the kind considered back in Chapter 2. But the interpretation Milosz offers—which is actually a kind of causal explanation—is curious and worth questioning. It was his relative's fault, he tells us; there was a concrete origin, an event, that turned him into a boy possessed of hurtful abstractions, which had happened his way as if by alien force. But Milosz may well be hunting in the wrong territory to make sense of things. It is certainly possible that there existed a concrete origin of the sort he posits; in this case, he will have functioned like a detective, who finally finds the missing piece to the puzzle at hand. I cannot help but wonder, however, whether the attitude with which he had carried his slingshot doesn't go deeper, beyond events and incidents, into the very texture of things.

On some level, perhaps, it doesn't matter. What is most important, one might argue, is the fact that the behavior has been identified, named. But whether the origin lies in his despised relative or in his polluted world matters a great deal to his own, and our own, understanding. One interpretation brings us an essentially psychological account of a bit of bad behavior. The other brings us into the heart of history. Given Milosz's stated aims, the account he has given us is somewhat anomalous; he seems to have done what he told us he would try to refrain from doing. But this itself, I would suggest, bespeaks his own formation as a modern autobiographical subject, trying, against difficult odds, to move beyond the confines of the monadic self to tell a different kind of story.

As Patricia Hampl has noted in an essay (1999) on Milosz's work, he has crafted a method "which allows the self to function not as a source or a subject"—or not *only* as a source or subject—"but as an instrument for rendering the world" (p. 86). What a story like his shows is that "we embody, if unwittingly and partially, our history, even our prehistory. The past courses through our veins. The self is the instrument which allows us not only to live this truth but to contemplate it" (p. 97). As Hampl goes on to suggest, this form of contemplative remembering exemplified in Milosz's autobiography is, perhaps,

> closer to poetry than to fiction, in spite of the apparent narrative affinity of the novel and autobiography, and in spite of the autobiographical nature of much modern fiction. In the lyric poem and the memoir, a self speaks, renders the world, or is recast in its image. In both lyric poetry and the memoir the real subject is consciousness in the light of history. The ability to transmit the impulses of the age, the immediacy of a human life moving through the changing world, is common to both genres. To be personal and impersonal all at once is the goal of both. (p. 100)

In this respect, autobiographical understanding, as it emerges in hindsight via narrative reflection, has history at its very core.

Deep Identity

In his reflections on the supra-personal dimensions of self-formation, the philosopher Alasdair MacIntyre reminds us that, "I inherit from the past of my family, my city, my tribe, my nation, a variety of debts, inheritances, rightful expectations and obligations. These constitute the given of my life, my moral starting point. This is in part what gives my life its own moral particularity" (1981, p. 205). As MacIntyre goes on to note,

> This thought is likely to appear alien and even surprising from the standpoint of modern individualism. From the standpoint of individualism I am what I myself choose to be. I can always, if I wish to, put in question what are taken to be the merely contingent social features of my existence. I may biologically be my father's son; but I cannot be held responsible for what he did unless I choose implicitly or explicitly to assume such responsibility. I may legally be a citizen of a certain country; but I cannot be held responsible for what my country does or has done unless I choose implicitly or explicitly to assume such responsibility. (p. 205)

We are here considering an attitude, MacIntyre explains, "according to which the self is detachable from its social and historical roles and statuses" (p. 205).

But this attitude is cast radically into question by experiences of the sort considered in this chapter. To refer to MacIntyre once more:

> The story of my life is always embedded in those communities from which I derive my identity. I am born with a past; and to try to cut myself off from that past, in the individualist mode, is

to deform my present relationships. The possession of an historical identity and the possession of a social identity coincide. . . .
What I am, therefore, is in key part what I inherit, a specific past
that is present to some degree in my present. I find myself part of
a history and that is generally to say, whether I like it or not,
whether I recognise it or not, one of the bearers of a tradition.
(pp. 205–206)

It is the phrase "whether I recognise it or not" that is of
central importance. Many aspects of my historical inheritance
are conscious or preconscious, able to be brought to mind
given the right circumstances. But some are *un*conscious,
which is to say they refer to those deep strata of history of
which I may be largely, if not entirely, unaware. So it is that I
earlier spoke of the narrative unconscious in reference to those
culturally rooted aspects of one's history that have not yet
become part of one's story. They are hidden, not so much in
the sense of that which has been buried through the forceful
work of repression, as that which remains unthought and is
thus not yet a part of the story I can tell. I would suggest
further that this "hiddenness" is one of the legacies of modernity, or at least that aspect of it that, through the fashioning
of the sovereign individual, ostensibly free to choose his or her
own way, effectively erases from view those historical and
cultural moorings that are the very ground of identity.
Taking this idea one step farther, it might be said that the
modern self, for all of its memoirs and autobiographies, is a
self that is in large measure unconscious of its own historical
formation. Indeed, it is perhaps the very widening and
deepening of the narrative unconscious that is the precondi-
tion of the modern autobiographical project, predicated as it
is on the presumption that it is the unique and unrepeatable

characteristics of one's life that are most worthy of being recounted.

As the sociologist Edward Shils (1981) adds, "Every human action and belief has a career behind it; it is the momentary end-state of a sequence of transmissions and modifications and their adaptation to current circumstances. Although everyone bears a great deal of past achievement in his belief and conduct, there are many persons who fail to see this" (p. 43). Putting a bit more of a positive spin on these issues than MacIntyre, Shils acknowledges that

> It was a great achievement of moral and political philosophy to postulate the existence of a self-contained human being as a self-determining moral entity free from original sin and from the toils of a dark inheritance. The ideal was to expunge from human beings all that came from the past and hindered their complete self-regulation and expression. . . . Much progress has been made in this regard. But it has its limits. There are undoubtedly many persons who regard their pasts as beginning only with their own birth. They believe that it lies within their powers to order entirely their own existence by their "own" decisions and those of their contemporaries. (pp. 43–44)

These are individuals "whose 'organ' or sense of the past is wholly empty," Shils argues, "and they are wrong as well" (p. 44). If Shils is right, the modern autobiographical subject, whose past appears limited to his or her own life, is something of a *mistake*.

What is important to emphasize is that Shils actually seems to be talking about *memory* in this context. "The individual as he perceives himself includes things which are not bounded by his own experiences" (1981, p. 50). The fabric of memory, he goes on to say, "is furnished not only from the recollections of events which the individual has himself experienced but from the memories of others. . . . From their accounts of their own experiences, which frequently antedate his own, and from written works at various removes, his image of his 'larger self' is brought to include events which occurred both recently and earlier outside his own experiences" (p. 51). What Shils seems to be suggesting, therefore, is that history, in all of its variousness as it operates within the individual, is itself a *part* of memory. The notion that it must be confined to one's life-span is therefore being challenged, radically.

One significant implication, then, is that perhaps we need to think about memory in a new way. As the philosopher Hans-Georg Gadamer (1975) puts the matter, "It is time to rescue the phenomenon of memory from being regarded merely as a psychological faculty and to see it as an essential element in the finite historical being of man" (p. 16). One might speak of *deep memory* in this context. In a related vein, we might think about self and identity in a new way as well. For, alongside our manifest identity, our conscious sense of who and what we are, is what might be termed our *deep identity*, by which I refer to those dimensions of identity that find their origins not in the personal particulars of a life but in the fabric of history. Finally, there is the need to think anew about narrative reflection and autobiographical understanding. "Self-reflection and autobio-graphy," Gadamer reminds us, "are not primary . . . through them history is made private once more." My history, indeed "my life," is not mine alone. "In fact," Gadamer insists, "history does not belong to us, but we belong to it" (p. 245).

From the perspective outlined in this chapter, autobiography is no longer a matter—or no longer exclusively a matter—of representing a life, from birth until death. Instead, it is a matter of discerning, as best one can, the multiple sources, both near and far, that give rise to the self. This does not eliminate the place of the "I" in telling the self's story. The project at hand—whether it takes place intentionally, as in the writing of an autobiography, or unintentionally, as in the course of reflection—is, again, one of *poiesis,* of fashioning an identity in and through these multiple sources.[6] But this very dimension of *poiesis* is itself a part of history, as are the genres and storylines employed in the task.

In much of my recent work I have tried to show that narrative, rather than being imposed on life from without, is woven into the very fabric of experience.[7] In line with this aim, part of what I have tried to show in this chapter is that there are narrative "reserves," untold and unwritten stories, cultural as well as personal, that are in important respects constitutive of experience and identity. Narratives are with us in ways we don't quite know; they are part of our deep memory, as I have called it, which is itself comprised, in part, of sedimented layers of history. By recognizing this via the reflective work of hindsight, we open ourselves to the possibility of exploring new and different forms of making sense of personal life.

---

[6] Freeman, 1999, 2002b, 2002c.
[7] For example, 1997a, 1997b.

FIVE

NARRATIVE FORECLOSURE

THE WEIGHT OF THE PAST

In Chapter 3, which explored Primo Levi's *The Drowned and the Saved* (1989), I focused on the idea of "moral lateness" and tried to show how, via hindsight, a measure of recollective "rescue" could occur. In looking back on his past, Levi had become able to see certain things about himself and about humanity that he had been unable to see, or see clearly, earlier on. In one sense, the process was freeing: through the distant perch of hindsight, he could free himself from the oblivion of the chaotic moment. In another sense, however, the process had resulted in a kind of imprisonment: the sins he had come to believe he committed could not be undone and hung about him like a dead weight. In Chapter 4, we saw in operation another kind of weight, namely, the one imposed by history. Until she had begun in earnest the project of narrative reflection, Eva Hoffman told us, it hadn't occurred to her that she was "in effect a receptacle of a historical legacy, or that its burden had a significance and weight that needed to be acknowledged." So it was that personal memory had come to be linked to "a larger history," such that "the heavy dimensions of this inheritance started becoming fully apparent" (2002, p. x).

In this chapter, I try to draw these two strands of thought together by showing how the weight of history—the frequently unacknowledged shaping forces that one may carry within— can become the sort of immovable prison we had observed in the case of Primo Levi. There is much indeed that we carry within us from history and culture. We are told how to live and who to be, what our possibilities are and our limits, and these "instructions" and expectations—especially when unacknow- ledged—can become every bit as paralyzing as the conviction that the sins of the past can never be undone. In situations such as these, hindsight can provide a vehicle for opening up the story of the past, and it does so precisely to the degree that it can reveal the profound ways in which the weight of history, both personal and supra-personal, has been operative in our formation.

In the pages to follow, I focus on two artists, "Samuel" and "Leah," who experience what I call *narrative foreclosure,* the conviction that the story of one's life, or life work, has effectively ended.[1] At an extreme, narrative foreclosure may lead to a kind of living death or even suicide, the presumption being that the future is a foregone conclusion, an inevitable reiteration of one's present suffering or paralysis. There is some indication that Primo Levi had fallen victim to this deadly path and that its motivation may have had something to do with the conviction that he could never free himself from the enormity of his past and that it would haunt him evermore. Narrative foreclosure is also at work when, as we will see with Samuel, one carries the unshak- able conviction that it is simply too late to live meaningfully and

---

[1] See Freeman, 2000a.

that, consequently, there is little left to do but play out the prescripted ending. The phenomenon of aging, particularly in modern Western culture, readily comes to mind in this context: with prescripted narratives of decline well in place, there frequently appears little choice among the aged but to reconcile themselves to their narrative fate. We thus encounter once more the narrative unconscious, albeit in somewhat different form than we encountered it in the previous chapter: as "natural" as it may seem to avow, to oneself and others, that one's story is essentially over, this very avowal is, in significant part, a function of what has been internalized, unknowingly, from the cultural-historical surround. This conviction is often not the individual's alone. It may be a cultural one as well, tied to prevailing images of growth and decline or to the existence of cultural institutions that either fail to support the continued renewal of the life story or actively promote its premature ending. In this respect, narrative foreclosure may also be related more generally to the reification of cultural storylines and the tendency, on the part of some, to internalize these storylines in such a way as to severely constrict their own field of narrative expression: the story goes this way, not that.

Leah's story recounts the emergence of a different possibility, a different response altogether to the potential paralysis of narrative foreclosure. She is an artist who, upon arriving at what can only be called an artistic point of no return, was able to call a halt to the story she had been living and eventually create a new one, in which she herself had a greater measure of freedom and control. She too had internalized certain salient cultural storylines, with the result that, for a time, she had been rendered artistically "mute," effectively silenced by the strange and untenable conditions within which she had been trying to create.[2] The question that she

---

[2] See Freeman, 2000b.

ultimately had to address was whether there was enough to sustain her in her efforts to move forward. As we shall see, there was: in the face of what had seemed to be the point of no return, she gathered what she could of her own artistic resources and learned how to speak once more. By following the contours of her story, perhaps we can gain some insight into the process by which the spell of narrative foreclosure may be broken. Hindsight will play a key role in the process once again. Narrative reflection, however, will be assuming a somewhat different form than what we have encountered thus far, one involving *demystification* of the storylines one has unwittingly internalized (see especially Ricoeur, 1970, 1974; Josselson, 2004). This can be difficult indeed, precisely because these storylines, in their pervasiveness and seeming "naturalness," constitute the very medium in which we live. "This is the way things are," we might say. This is what it means to grow old, to be an artist, to be a man or a woman. Images and storylines congeal, harden, and become solidified—so much so that the future may appear utterly foreordained. This condition of narrative foreclosure calls for a special form of narrative reflection, one that not only re-views past understandings and thinks them anew but seeks to discern how these understandings came into being and why they had been so mystifying. By making the narrative unconscious conscious, the spell of narrative foreclosure may be broken and the future opened once more.

DEAD ENDS

In his mid-60s when he was interviewed for a research project of which I was a part,[3] Samuel is a man who had considerable

---

[3] The case history information used in this chapter was gathered as part of a research project funded by the Spencer and MacArthur Foundations, conducted at The University of Chicago under the direction of Mihaly Csikszentmihalyi, J.W. Getzels, and Stephen P. Kahn.

difficulty doing the kind of art that he believed he could be doing and who, in the process of narrating the story of his life over the course of the last 20 or so years, adduced numerous reasons for his troubles. His past, once a source of pleasure and pride, becomes a source of pain and shame; his own apparent ending—his anticipated failure to become the artist he had dreamed of becoming—leads to a pervasive sense of despair, which in turn taints the story he tells of his past. He is convinced that the glories of the past were, perhaps, not so glorious after all, that they were in fact illusory and said more about his grandiose fantasies than his real achievements. In his eyes, it was simply impossible for something so glorious to have culminated in something so grim. Recall what Primo Levi had said about the emotional consequences of the punishment he and his comrades had received in the concentration camps: "if there is punishment, there must have been guilt" (1989, p. 76). The logic in Samuel's case is much the same: if there is the nothingness of narrative foreclosure, there must have been little there to begin with. Notice here that the problem isn't foreclosure alone; it is that the past has been poisoned and indeed falsified by virtue of the outcome and apparent ending-to-be.

Prior to attending art school in the early 1960s, Samuel had worked as an editor for a publishing company in a large city. While in art school, he worked part-time, but resumed full-time responsibilities upon graduating from art school in 1964 at the age of 45. Several years later, he moved with his new wife to the small town she was from, which promised to be a great place to settle, raise a family perhaps, and do some serious painting. Despite the fact that his new home was about three hours from the city, Samuel chose not to give up his editorial job; the long commute and the hassle involved in staying with friends in the city for several days during the work week weren't so arduous as to incite him to leave. The job remained important, both financially and emotionally; it was the one place, he said, where he was truly needed.

Not surprisingly, however, he had grown more and more to feel that his life was dominated by the logistical difficulties of keeping a job so far away from his home. Although he continued to maintain a studio in the city, he felt that he was virtually unable to do anything creative while he was there; it was too unsettled, too temporary. "I've always felt displaced. When I'm in [the city], either I have to chat it up with whoever I'm staying with or there are other distractions. . . . I've never been able to do anything really creative in that city since I left. . . . It's always been a temporary situation. So I don't do anything." The other problem simply had to do with his energy level. After a hard day's work, it was difficult to turn to his art even in the country, particularly since he was getting on in years; he was tired and needed his rest. "When I leave here," therefore, referring to his home in the country, "I'm artistically dead."

When he had lived in the city, Samuel had had a number of paintings in shows, had established a solid gallery connection, and had even won a prize for his work. With his move, however, he was just too far away to remain actively involved with the art scene. In the country, he had been fortunate to establish a gallery connection not too long after his arrival. But after some six or seven years, the gallery had been forced to go out of business, leaving him empty-handed. By the time of the interview, the art market, by his account at any rate, had become dismal. "For various reasons, this is a terrible area to sell anything more than a watercolor. . . . If you do watercolors and representational, small things, you can make a living at that—in other words, what I consider more in the realm of commercial art." But not much more could be done out there.

The locals' artistic appreciation was "nil," he explained; as for the visitors who would occasionally come through town on their country outings, they were unlikely to shell out money for such an unknown quantity as him. "It's too chancy."

As he continued to reflect on this situation, the picture darkened further. He recounted an opening he had had some time ago, when the rain was coming down so hard that only four or five people showed up. "I remember we had a lot of bottles of champagne left," he said. When it came right down to it, though, he went on to say, this opening wasn't much different from those that went on when the weather was just fine, and in bigger venues than this one. Many years back there had been another opening, at a well-known art center: "It was one of those clever shows. . . . It was a black and white show—only black and white sculpture and painting and so on. And if you wanted, you could dress up in a black and white costume, that sort of thing." It had been a lot of fun. Shortly after, a critic had written "that it was as if the world of art, that particular night, was centered [right there]. . . . And of course it wasn't at all. I mean that people there had the feeling that this was important. But frankly, nobody gave a damn two blocks away, I'm sure."

Judging by his words, Samuel had come to find it increasingly difficult to see his former excitement as real. Despite the incredible sense of possibility these openings had once presented, he knew now that they would lead nowhere. And so, despite a shared conviction at the time among him and his fellow artists that "this was where it was at," it proved to be an "illusion." His past thus appeared foolish to him, inflated with the grandiosity of youth. The reality, he suggested, was that he and his friends had gotten caught up in the moment. And the problem was that this moment was nothing short of mythical, or so it appears in retrospect: artists, on the move, living the high life, their futures

wide open, there for the asking. Whatever joy and exuberance
there had been had now become bathed in the bleakness of the
situation in which he had landed. Like so many others, his plans
had been "to do a lot of painting, and attract a gallery, and be
some kind of an artistic success." But apparently, it wasn't
meant to be.

Commenting again on those people in his home town who
do "pretty little watercolors," he said, "More power to them. If
this is what truly makes them happy, I envy them, I truly envy
them." But "it's not for me." He also envied "the person who
can produce a real good body of important work and not have
any encouragement, do this on his own and plug away." The
people he envied most, however, were artists like Picasso,
Braque, and Chagall, "who, aside from the commercial success
they all achieved . . . were able to do what they really want to do
superbly—you know, to find themselves. . . . I don't care when
you find it, whether you're a Giorgione who dies of the plague at
31 or 33, who finds it early and dies early, or whether you find it
when you're 60 . . . or whether you're somewhere in the middle
and lose it. But you've had it. At least you've been there." As for
himself, it was unlikely that he would ever meet with such good
fortune. "I'm distracted," he said again. "I allow myself to be
distracted, I think, because I'm afraid I'm never going to find
it." Although he never quite said what "it" was, we can presume
that he was referring to that sort of soulful artistic stride so
integral to the romantic image of the artist—the Artist/God,
seeking against all odds to locate within the interior of the self
the deep pulse of things.

As Samuel went on to explain, his plight was hardly unique.
Artists like Braque and Chagall, he noted, "touched brush to
canvas and they knew basically where they were going. . . . They
already had a road map in their mind, and it was just a matter of

kind of working out the details, moving a certain amount of furniture around, so to speak, like the old religious painters of the 13th and 14th centuries." But "it wasn't that simple for the modern artist. . . . After Picasso, what is there left to do? In other words, it's all been done." As for those who came before Picasso and company—painters like Rembrandt, Velazquez, and Titian—the story is even more disturbing. Again, "what is there left to do? "It's been done and it's been done superbly well by these people hundreds of years ago, and it's been done superbly by Picasso fifty years ago or sixty years ago. So let's not talk about that; let's do some paper clips, something Picasso never thought of doing." There is "an element of nihilism" involved in the current art scene, he believed, and "a certain element of despair" as well. "I detect it already from conversations with instructors and contemporary artists. I mean, big deal; it's all been done; so what's new? That's the way I feel." Samuel's search for himself and his art had become desperate. He described himself as looking frantically for that elusive formula—that magical "it" others had been able to "find"— which would allow him to gather both the creativity and the recognition that might have accrued to him at some other time or place. Now, as always, he was "trying to find some new way," but like so many of his artistic forays to date, they each turned out to be "less an avenue than a blind alley."

Whether perceived or real, the dilemma at hand had left Samuel virtually paralyzed. The ideal condition for creativity, Samuel said, is "where art isn't beholden to any commercial considerations, where you don't have to make a living at it, where you don't have to please a customer, where you don't have to please a dictator." If it wasn't for the lingering gaze of the public eye, in other words, the situation for artists like himself would be vastly improved. There would be no rules, no dictates;

they would able to remain true to their own hearts. But then, of course, there would still remain the plight of the modern artist, left to his own solitary devices, without rules, dictates, "road maps." The dilemma, therefore, was that if artists painted expressly for others, as he had sometimes done, the creative process would inevitably be deformed; by acquiescing to their demands and desires, one couldn't help but falsify art's True Meaning. At the same time, if artists created strictly for themselves, without attending to what the public considered legitimate or valid, they would be left in a kind of vacuum, devoid both of encouragement and those sorts of enduring traditions that, in his estimation, had once allowed them to carry out their work with a much greater sense of certainty and security. "The contemporary artist," he went on to ask again, "what does he have?" The answer: "He doesn't have anything really; he has to find his own way."

The implication is an interesting, if familiar, one. In some sense, Samuel had implied that the entire art world could be characterized by a kind of narrative foreclosure, the postmodern era representing for some "the end of art," the playing-out of a history previously grounded in tradition but now in the process of succumbing to a vertiginous free-for-all, where it was every man—and men were certainly the dominant players at this time—for himself. For many artists (Samuel harped repeatedly on Claes Oldenburg, with his flaccid sculptures of outsize paper clips, among other soft, mundane things), this would mean ceaseless repetition of one's brand image and could only yield tedium. As for himself, Samuel suggested, it meant a mad dash for the fashioning of his own artistic identity, his own unique and unrepeatable Self. His goals as an artist were modest ones, he insisted. "At my age I'd like to make a little ripple in the art world, certainly," he said. But, "I don't think it would be realistic to expect it." Subjectively speaking, it was too late; judging by what he "knew" about the process of aging, he was past his prime and thus all but finished. Even after all those years, he confessed, "I don't know who the real me is. I don't know if I will ever know." Alongside the storyline of the Artist/ God in search of "it" is the storyline of the Wandering Self in search of the "real me," teasingly out of reach for those without the inner resources required. What made things more frantic still was the fact that, in his eyes, time was running out.

Mystification and Demystification

It should be emphasized that this man had remained excited by the process of painting, by handling paint and seeing what it could do on a canvas. But he was no longer able to experience his involvement in painting as part of an ongoing project, as a narrative with some promise of continuing. By all indications, his work could not possibly contribute to the future, which had already been sealed shut, or at least virtually so; it was only part of a perpetual present, leading nowhere. From his perspective, the very factors that might allow his "search" to lead *somewhere* were simply not operative in the world he had come to inhabit. Perhaps this is why his past, as he reconstructs it, is characterized less by a series of meaningfully interconnected episodes than by a series of fits and starts, movements in this direction and then that, all of which are permeated by the countless distractions upon which he can seize in order, temporarily, to prevent himself from gazing into the abyss.

Samuel's predicament is a painful one. On the one hand, the very doubt of there emerging a significant ending, now exacerbated by his conviction in his own inevitable failure, leads to the fashioning of a narrative that, for all of its mini-triumphs and good times, cannot help but appear to be an exercise in futility and, on some level, delusion: that was a silly man back there, so filled with his own fantasies that he had mistaken them for realities. The good times *couldn't* have been that good, therefore; if they had been, they would have led somewhere better than here. All that might have been truly worthwhile, or that had at least appeared to be, has gotten swallowed up by what has followed in its path. On the other hand, there simultaneously emerges the conviction that maybe, after all is said and done, there just hadn't been much there to begin with. Even as the present discolors the past, the past—now perhaps being seen, a la Ivan Ilych for what it really was, namely an illusory and somewhat masochistic exercise in futility—has yielded a present, and in turn a future, largely devoid of form. Only a would-be story is left to be told, not an actual one, of the sort he had wished to tell. Narrative foreclosure brings in its wake the loss of narrative itself. There can be no story without an ending, and there can be no ending without a story.

Part of Samuel's artistic immobility undoubtedly derived from his own inflated images of the artist. When asked to reflect on the artist's place in society, he expressed the belief that "the artist is one of the principal reasons that mankind is here. When I hear about people making a lot of money or inventing marvelous labor-saving devices or whatever," he explained, "I say that's all well and good. But all that is a high animal level. . . . You're not rolling around in the mud; you're not living in a cave. Say you're living in a mansion, and you might have nice things even. But the artist is what it's all about, in my opinion. It's the culmination of mankind; it's the flame. . . . The artist to me is God-like. He's the Prometheus pulling down the fire." Given these sentiments, it is little wonder that Samuel was doubtful about his own future and its prospects. He was no "God," and the odds were against his ever becoming one.

Another part of Samuel's artistic immobility surely had to do with the multiplicity of factors, from the local to the epochal, that, by his own account, had conspired to freeze him in his artistic tracks. Alongside his geographical isolation was the isolation that inevitably befell those modern artists who, like himself, were destined to remain "adrift," left to their own meager devices in a world devoid not only of meaningful artistic traditions but of *care* for what artists did. "This isn't the era of the artist," he complained at one point. "This is the era of the engineer, the technician." Yes, he had to admit, maybe someone who was "extremely gifted" or a "wealthy dilettante" could pursue a lifetime career in fine art; he knew that there were people who had been able to make a go of it. But "Art can be a real burden to those of us who have not supreme ability or supreme pushiness or supreme good luck or a combination to excel in 'real' terms." They were forced to "move ahead without very much outside help, direction, or interest."

These two storylines—the first focusing on Samuel's mythical images of the Artist/God, the second focusing on the beleaguered victim of modernity, hopelessly captive to the dizziness of freedom, the shallowness of the masses, and the mechanical whir of the epoch—had found their way into what I have been calling the narrative unconscious. Indeed, he had internalized these storylines in such a way that they came to inhabit him, to pervade his every move. Whether they finally amounted to excuses, defenses designed to assuage the fact that he had been the architect of his own destiny, is largely immaterial; psychically speaking, the weight of these realities was massive. So too, I would suggest, was the weight of his own self-perception as a man growing old, staring in the face of his own inevitable failure, his own inability ever to measure up to the idealized images that had peopled his imagination. Interestingly enough, he claimed to have retained a measure of hope through it all: "Where there's life there's hope," he had said. "I don't think all is lost." But it was not at all clear what he could possibly do, at this moment of his life, to move forward.

Although Samuel himself made only the most oblique references to it, it can plausibly be argued that, alongside the storylines identified thus far, yet another one had come to inhabit him, more surreptitiously—and more perniciously—than all the rest. I am referring to that sort of story which is, in effect, a *non*-story, one that is so thoroughly devoid of possible future episodes as to lose direction and momentum. We might think of the process of reading works of literature in this context, focusing especially on the dimension of hindsight. Often, it is only after we have finished reading that we are able to understand why things happened as they did; the ending reverberates backward, serving to provide a measure of interpretive closure to what had previously been fundamentally open. A corollary exists here as well. And that is, if we already know, or believe we know, the ending of the work ahead of time, there may be little motivation to continue reading; whether rightly or wrongly, we may become convinced that there is little more to be had by lasting until the very end. It might be said, then, that Samuel is both a writer and a reader who believes he knows how the "work" that is his life will end. Far from being the blaze of glory he had hoped for, there will be ashes of disappointment, regret, and shame. This failed ending he envisions for himself magnifies his inability to create, both as an artist and a person. Indeed, functionally speaking, the inability to create is one way in which the idea of narrative foreclosure may be operationalized: insofar as the final chapter of one's life is a foregone conclusion, one can no longer move creatively into the future. The only story to be told is the one that is over.

I earlier suggested that narrative foreclosure may be defined as the premature conviction that one's life story has effectively ended: there is no more to tell; there is no more that *can* be told. For some people, there is little to lament about this situation. For those like Samuel, however, narrative foreclosure brings in tow the futility of seeking to contribute to a future the meaning of which has already been determined. It is therefore the death of narrative desire, the shutting-down of the possibility of there ever emerging a different ending than the one envisioned now. The question is: What might one do in such a situation? More precisely, what can be done to "reopen" a foreclosed narrative of the sort presented here?

Insofar as one's view of the future conditions the meaning of the past, there exists the need to reimagine, indeed to *rewrite,* the future. For Samuel and others like him, the fixed nature of the present is such that the future, the seemingly inevitable victim of repetition, becomes closed off. In some way or other, therefore, the chains of the present must loosen their hold. This process appeared unavailable to Samuel; he was held too tightly in the mythical stories he had internalized to break their spell; at the "ripe old age," as he had put it, of 63, he seemed to feel that he was on the way out. In part, this was surely his own problem, a function of his own self-perceived limits. At the same time, the forces at work extend well beyond the boundaries of the sovereign self. Narrative foreclosure, in cases like these, is not to be framed in purely individual terms; it is an eminently social phenomenon, brought about, in some instances at any rate, by people having been unwittingly relegated, by the images and discourses surrounding them, to the status of the living dead. Some, were they made aware of this problem, may elect to live their lives in much the same way; they simply may not be bothered by the supposition that their lives have effectively ended. Or, they may not feel that their lives have ended at all; they have just changed, in a certain way. Others, however, may seek to call a halt to their own "self-determinism," in the hope of fashioning somewhat different ends, and endings, than the one they had envisioned. Hence the importance of rewriting the future.

Just as the future must be rewritten in order to break the stranglehold of narrative foreclosure, so too must the past. The first, very difficult step in doing so is *demystification*; that is, one must become more consciously aware of the scripts and story-lines one has internalized. Like Samuel, for example, many artists have become the unwitting hosts of the artist's mystique and its associated storylines during the course of recent decades, with the result that the pursuit of their work has been sacrificed to the pursuit of an image—most often, either of the Artist/God or of the struggling, beleaguered hermit, holed up in a garret, hungry and alone but free.[4] Only when these artists were able to identify how these storylines had been operative in their own lives, how they had taken them unawares, did it become pos-sible for them to carry out their artistic activities in less alienated fashion. The first step of demystification, therefore, consists precisely in acknowledging one's own mystification, one's own condition of being inhabited by scripts and storylines so pervasive as to be mistaken for the natural order of things. Upon doing so, one can begin to undo them, loosen their hold.

[4] My book *Finding the Muse: A Sociopsychological Inquiry into the Conditions of Artistic Creativity* (1994), provides an in-depth exploration of this and other pervasive "myths" about artists and their work.

In a related vein, a process of *desocialization* must occur as well, and it essentially involves identifying those ways in which one has been constructed as a social agent and carrier of culture and, in doing so, beginning to move beyond them. This process is another way of speaking about making the unconscious conscious, and it is at one and the same time a process of *reconstruction,* of refashioning the past and thereby achieving some measure of self-renewal. Along these lines, one way Samuel might have been able to mobilize himself as an artist would have been through identifying the ways in which his own larger-than-life images of the artist had permeated his desires and through turning to different stories, different ways of emplotting the movement of his life. By making the narrative unconscious conscious, in other words, there might have emerged the opportunity to rewrite his story and, in turn, his self.

BEYOND FORECLOSURE

Let us now turn to Leah, a woman who did ultimately manage to break the spell of narrative foreclosure. Like many others in the group of artists with whom we spoke, she had been immersed in her younger years in an art scene that had been terrifically exciting. As a member of a well-known group of artists who shared many of her artistic ideas and aims, she had been able to gain entry into the art world in a way that was comparatively problem-free. It had been "a lovely way to begin showing. It was very low pressure, we were full of piss and vinegar, thought we were the hottest shit on earth." Not too long after this period, however, things would become decidedly "more serious"; "[it] began with the selling and the commercial galleries, and who got galleries and who didn't." Sadness set in, she noted. "I recognized that some of the joy of the work was over." The gallery scene aside, Leah had also grown uncomfortable with some of the art she was doing. However much she may have benefited from being a member in good standing in a notable, indeed notorious, group of like-minded others, she had come to question the work itself, especially the boisterous imagery that had become the group's trademark. For this reason, she said, "I began working against everything I learned in school." She wanted to do her own work and form her own artistic identity; and to do so, she realized, she would have to interrogate and lay bare the most elemental sources of her art.

Upon rejecting the loud, imagistic art she done before, she turned her attention to how paintings were constructed, how colors and canvas, working together, came to acquire meaning and power. Her work therefore became much more formal and "reductive," as she put it. The process, at this juncture, was one of "elimination," one in which she would continue removing from her work anything and everything that was *un*necessary in order to determine what was—that is, in order to determine what paintings required for their very existence. Valuable though this process of eliminative stripping-down had been, it had also yielded a painful and disturbing realization: were she to continue in this reductive mode of painting, there ultimately might be nothing left at all. In a distinct sense, Leah had come to realize that *nothing* was essential, that there *was* no foundation or ground for a painting's existence, no identifiable set of ingredients or qualities that would proclaim its necessity. Along these lines, perhaps there was no identifiable reason for her, or anyone else, to paint. Here she was, creating essentially useless objects that had no discernible rationale, no reason for being. Should she continue trying to create art? Was she an artist? An artistic breakdown eventually would occur. She would be rendered mute, reduced to silence.

How did this happen? How *could* it happen? She had once been so passionate about painting and about being an artist. Could it be that all of that passion and sense of purpose was an artifact of the narratives that had been in circulation at the time, about the rapturous, rebellious world of the modern artist, free to do her thing? She would have to interrogate her reductive phase in much the same way, for it was distinctly possible that her seemingly earnest desire to get to the heart of art's bare essentials was as much a product of prevailing storylines—in this case about the deconstruction of art's sacred essence, even the very end of art—as that earlier passion. Given her confusion and uncertainty, only one thing was really left to do: she had to ask herself, as honestly as she could, whether there was enough in the experience of painting to warrant her continuing.

As harrowing as Leah's questioning process had been, the answer turned out to be straightforward. Through it all, she was an *artist,* and she would have to figure out a way of reconnecting herself to those aspects of painting that she had once found so captivating and real. "It became a process," she explained, "of accepting the tradition of painting and introducing additive thinking." The first paintings she did after this turnabout "looked almost as reductive as the work which preceded it." But "there was a different construct underlying it," a different sense of what it was all about.

Much of the work in her reductive phase, she went on to say, had been about perceptual "issues" that were being addressed in the art world. These were paintings that "the eye scanned in a certain way." But there was something "manipulative" about these paintings, she had come to feel, and they simply weren't having the kind of deeply felt impact that she had once believed, in her heart, paintings ought to have. Leah had also grown less interested in addressing intellectual issues in her work. It used to be important to her, she said, "to have a kind of intellectual control" over her painting and to be "capable of addressing certain issues," so that "if someone said that this was a particular critical issue in the air at that moment, in some way or other the painting dealt with that, whether by ignoring it or tackling it or working against it." Things were different now. "I just don't care about those issues anymore." In her own eyes, she had become a kind of accomplice to an overly intellectualized approach to creating art, one that had been foisted upon her and that had taken her unawares. It was only now, after the fact, that she could see what exactly had happened. And it was only now, upon this seeing, that she could begin to do something more real, more in tune with her true interests and passions. Her work would eventually become "operatic," as she put it, "inclusive of everything I know that seems appropriate for that painting." Each one would be "more or less its own entity"; it would define its own terms rather than be defined ahead of time by some art world–driven idea about art or perception or reality. The goal was simple: "I want to do a really good painting."

Among the many things Leah had learned during the course of her artistic breakdown and subsequent return to painting was that she was "still a romantic" who was committed to doing expressive work. Even during her reductive phase, the desire to express had been there. In her "heart of hearts," in fact, she was most at home with the work of the abstract expressionists. She could do without their angst, and she was not interested in that self-indulgent and self-destructive form of "male heroic" that frequently came with their work. But she very much admired their passion and expressive engagement with their work, as well as their refusal to be seduced by the latest art world ideas and issues.

Some of these ideas and issues would occasionally surface still, Leah admitted, and suspicion and doubt would come her way once again. "There are always points when it seems to be going well, and I think I'm this great genius and everything's wonderful and I'm in love with myself and the painting and the world and everything else. There are other points," however, "when I hate myself, the painting, the world, everything else." Looking backward, she would surely hate her own self-love as well, her own self-deluded rapture. All this was simply part of the territory. "Any work that is truly large, that is not task-oriented—which my work was for a couple of years—just includes the whole hubris and everything else." It also includes *doubt;* it is "simply part of it on one level," an intrinsic aspect of modern art and modern life. Not only were there no set criteria or "reasons" that could ever justify a painting's existence, there was also no way of ever knowing, definitively, whether a given work was any good or not; the criteria were too ambiguous and ephemeral. The challenge, therefore, was "to always measure your feeling against what you really do in the world." It was a difficult one, she quickly added. "It's very easy to give more credibility to doubt than one ought to." In the end, the only thing that could really save her—that *did* really save her—from being consumed by doubt was "the connection that periodically gets made between the material, the person doing it, and the thing being done, where it all fuses."

It was not an easy way of life, then or ever. "There is an interdependence with the world that there isn't in a more protected kind of position; you're more dependent on the world's good opinion." Perhaps this was why she had had to attend, carefully, to all of those art world issues in her younger days. There simply wasn't much "cushioning," as she put it. "We're organizing our own lives to some extent with a minimum of rules, and that's very scary stuff." What also made things hard, Leah added, is that "we're not wanted particularly." She and her fellow artists were often seen as little more than society's "irritants," and this too sometimes made it difficult to move forward in her life and work, feeling that it was all worthwhile.

For a time, in fact, she herself had become convinced that artists were "superfluous and useless." She had internalized the prevailing ethos regarding the primacy of "utilitarian value," with the result that she had become plagued by her own seemingly gratuitous existence. But this was a mistake; for even through all the anxiety and doubt that she and her fellow artists would endure, "We are not alienated workers." Art was only impotent to the extent that artists believed it to be—that is, to the extent that they capitulated to utilitarian values and applied them to their own work. What was necessary, therefore, she realized, was to refuse to buy into this crude utilitarian ethos. As she herself well knew, this was easier said than done. It was only in hindsight that she could see the measure of her own captivity. Not only had she herself, in her reductive, "task-oriented" phase, been an alienated worker; her alienation had been compounded by the supposition that she and her work were utterly useless. There is an ironic twist to her story: it was precisely during that phase that her work *was* useless, its reach extending only to those who were up on the latest issues. In this sense, her own suspicion and doubt had been all too well founded.

NARRATIVE FORCE AND NARRATIVE FREEDOM

Leah's burgeoning dissatisfaction with the art scene and her relationship to it had eventually led to her transformation as an artist. But it wasn't until the operatic opening in her work that she could see just how entrapped she had been by the lure of fame and fortune, by her own desire for recognition, and by the demands, both written and unwritten, that had been foisted upon her and that ultimately had much more to do with market value than human value. Some of what had gone on during those years had reached consciousness; it was impossible to be an up-and-coming New York artist and have no idea whatsoever about the art scene, market demands, and so on. But there had also been aspects of her history and her formation about which she had remained quite unconscious. She, like Samuel, had been living a life the contours of which owed their very existence to cultural discourses and storylines—to an element of *narrative force,* we might say—that she had yet to identify and name. Unlike Samuel, however, Leah had eventually managed to break the spell of narrative force and thereby set in motion her own narrative freedom—which is to say, the freedom to chart her own artistic and personal path.

In speaking of narrative freedom, I do not refer to some sort of sovereign, untrammeled state, in which one has become wholly released from the various influences and forces, narrative and otherwise, that permeate the life-world. This would be to extricate oneself from history itself; it would be to step out of the very medium in which we live. Nor do I wish to claim that the process of making the narrative unconscious conscious can be fully brought to completion; some aspects of our histories and our formation as subjects will always remain obscure, uncharted, indeed unconscious. In this respect, I would suggest once more that there is a basic and irreducible *alterity* that characterizes the human condition, an inner otherness and obscurity, founded upon our being "inhabited" by myriad influences, even forces, of which we are largely unaware.

This is hardly a new idea; for Freud, among others, it is the very centerpiece of human psychology. So too, of course, is the idea of the unconscious. As suggested in Chapter 4, however, the *narrative* unconscious is to be understood differently than the dynamic unconscious of which Freud and others have spoken. For it is a function not so much of repression, of the inadmissibility of fantasies and wishes, banished to the nether reaches of the psyche, as it is of our very existence as historical beings, living out stories that are only partly of our own making and about which we may be only partially conscious, if at all. For simplicity's sake, I have spoken of "the" narrative unconscious. Strictly speaking, this locution isn't quite right and bespeaks an aspect of substantiality—as if it were an entity, a discrete thing—that runs counter to my intention. In speaking of the narrative unconscious, therefore, I simply refer to those aspects of our histories about which we may be largely unaware and that have yet to become part of the stories we can tell about ourselves and how we came to be.

In Chapter 4, I focused mainly on those dimensions of "deep memory" and history that constitute what might in turn be called our "deep identities." These are elements of our identities from which we are not easily or readily freed, that indeed are bound to remain, to a greater or lesser extent, part of the very fabric of who we are—as women and men, as the inhabitants of particular nations and cultures, as actors in the living theater of history. In this chapter, I have focused mainly on those more "proximal" dimensions of memory and history that are tied to discrete cultural discourses and practices of the sort we find in particular fields of endeavor—in this case, art. I do not wish to erect a firm boundary between these two moments of the narrative unconscious; practically speaking, they are inseparable. But in the case of this more proximal arena of the narrative unconscious, there exists the possibility both of critique and liberation of a sort that is less readily attainable in the first.

While Samuel had remained ensnared in the workings of the narrative unconscious, the result being narrative foreclosure, Leah had managed to identify and name its covert operations and, in so doing, had "broken through" her own state of entrapment. Some aspects of her profile as an artist, she had discovered, were *not* fundamental to her deep identity, to her innermost sense of who and what she really was, but were instead extraneous and, at least in part, removable. These were elements of her identity and formation that she could critique and from which she could be freed. This freedom-from was the requisite condition for her freedom-to: her freedom to *create* in a manner she saw fit and to *live* in a manner that served to better actualize, strengthen, and extend her identity.

None of this could have transpired without the work of hindsight, which in Leah's case, more than in any of the others we have dealt with thus far, carried out the hermeneutically "suspicious" task of demystification. Some of Leah's motives, she had finally learned, had been superficial, even illusory. She had thus been a victim of false consciousness, broadly conceived, and the only way for her to move in the direction of true consciousness was to "unmask" these motives, to lay them bare. Doing so would prove to be arduous and painful; it is no small task to try to call a halt to one's inauthenticity and no small task to find, and live, another way. Samuel is an example of one who could not undertake the task. For him, hindsight proved to be particularly perilous, serving to poison his past; given where he had landed, as an artist and as an individual, it had become virtually impossible for him to look back on his earlier life with anything but disdain. It might be noted here that, generally speaking, autobiographical memory is seen as a source of self-aggrandizement, the tendency to paint the past in such a way as to create favorable, even if illusory, portraits of ourselves. As Samuel's story shows, however, the reconstructive process can work in the exact opposite direction as well. For him, hindsight had become the vehicle of his own self-diminution, the ultimate source being those storylines that had taken him unawares and had become constitutive of his very identity. In his case, therefore, the narrative unconscious continued to sustain narrative foreclosure and the repetition it had brought in tow. For Leah, hindsight operated very differently. Looking backward, she had eventually been able to make the narrative unconscious conscious; she had been able, that is, to see that she had unwittingly internalized narratives that had been destructive and paralyzing and that were more about art world fashions than they were about creating art. Only by making the narrative unconscious conscious, therefore, could she break the stranglehold of narrative foreclosure; and only then could she free herself to move authentically forward in her work and her life, hopeful that she was heading somewhere real.

THE VARIETIES OF UNCONSCIOUSNESS

In closing, I want to offer a brief qualification. I have been careful to distinguish the narrative unconscious from that form of the unconscious dealt with in psychoanalysis. I have also spoken of it mainly in relation to culture and history; that is, to discourses and forces outside the perimeter of the self, rather than in intrapsychic terms. It was for this reason that, in the case of both Samuel and Leah, I had underscored the importance of identifying and naming those cultural storylines that had so permeated their histories and identities as artists. This line of thinking should not, however, exclude the distinct possibility, even likelihood, that more dynamic intrapsychic factors generally associated with psychoanalytic thinking were also operative.

That Samuel had been colonized by prevailing storylines regarding the Artist/God seems unarguable. But it would be difficult to maintain that the shape his life had ultimately assumed was a function of these alone. By all indications, who he came to be had multiple origins, ranging from the farthest reaches of childhood all the way to those more proximal sources bound up with his adult life. There is no need to single out Samuel, however. For what has just been said about him surely applies in some measure to the lot of us. The alterity of the human condition has numerous sources indeed.

I noted in Chapter 3 that Freud himself was well aware of the importance of hindsight, as evidenced especially in his idea of "deferred action" (*Nachträglichkeit*). Back in 1895, he described a case of "a memory arousing an affect which it did not arouse as an experience, because in the meantime the change in puberty had made possible a different understanding of what was remembered" (1966, p. 356). In 1896, he also noted that "if [a] sexual experience occurs during a period of sexual immaturity and the memory of it is aroused during or after maturity, then the memory will have a far stronger excitatory effect than the experience did at the time it happened" (1962, p. 67). Although Freud didn't explicitly use the term hindsight to conceptualize these quite extraordinary discoveries—which, essentially, alerted him early on that human life could not adequately be understood via clock time or "charted" via the traditional if-then model of causality—he clearly recognized its power not only to reveal what had heretofore been inchoate or obscure but also to activate its causal energy. Earlier events, in effect, *became* causes retroactively, via hindsight. The psychoanalytic challenge, therefore, was not only to chart the movement of personal history in strict if-then fashion, as if the arrow of time pointed only forward, into the future; it was also to see how the meaning of events became reconstructed and refigured in line with present experience and continued development. Freud was thus well aware of the connection between hindsight and narrative as well: earlier experiences were to be understood as episodes in an evolving story, and this narrative work could only occur via hindsight, as one looked backward—with the help of the analyst, of course—and sought to discern the most basic sources of one's being.

Of more specific relevance to both the idea of the narrative unconscious and the interrelationship between it and narrative foreclosure are some of the ideas found in Freud's essay "Remembering, repeating, and working through" (1958 [1914]). Among some of his patients, prior to the emergence of certain memories, compulsive repetition would frequently occur—a kind of foreclosure in its own right. "We have learnt that the patient repeats instead of remembering," Freud writes, "and repeats under the conditions of resistance." As for what the patient repeats, "The answer is that he repeats everything that has already made its way from the sources of the repressed into his manifest personality—his inhibitions and unserviceable attitudes and his pathological character-traits." The challenge of treatment therefore consists largely of identifying the "state of illness" signified in the constellation of repeated symptoms being manifested and of "tracing it back to the past" (pp. 151–152). The process works in much the same way with narrative foreclosure in relation to the narrative unconscious: here too, a tracing-backward must occur, and here too it is necessary to undertake the task of making the unconscious conscious and thereby break the repetitive spell of foreclosure.

These two modes of unconsciousness overlap for a reason, and it has to do precisely with the nature of hindsight and the phenomenology of narrative time. Whether in the analytic setting or in the broader setting of "real life," coming to an understanding of oneself necessitates an interpretive process wherein past and present are disentangled and "disimplicated" from one another. Temporal distance is one vehicle for this process; by distancing oneself from the present moment, there sometimes emerges a measure of consciousness about what had heretofore been unconscious. Another vehicle is the sort of interpretive distancing found in therapeutic endeavors such as psychoanalysis. According to Freud,

> The main instrument . . . for curbing the patient's compulsion to repeat and for turning it into a motive for remembering lies in the handling of the transference [i.e., the patient's redirecting of feelings about others in the past toward the analyst]. We render the compulsion harmless, and indeed useful, by giving it the right to assert itself in a definite field. We admit it into the transference as a playground in which it is allowed to expand in almost complete freedom and in which it is expected to display to us everything in the way of pathogenic instincts that is hidden in the patient's mind. (p. 154)

This more secretive dimension of hiddenness, signified by resistance and founded in repression, differentiates the unconscious posited by Freud from the narrative unconscious that operates in narrative foreclosure. Both, however, place remembering—whether explicit or implicit—front and center; both involve "working through," in the sense of overcoming narrative force, whether externally generated or internally generated; both rely on a coming-to-light nurtured by distancing; and, perhaps most fundamentally, both involve the imaginative, poetic labor of narrative—specifically, the labor of reopening a narrative that had been stalled, frozen in its tracks. By thinking these two modes of unconsciousness together, as compatriots in the dialectic of self-understanding and self-renewal, we arrive at a more capacious and comprehensive picture of the role of hindsight in human affairs.

SIX

THE TRUTH OF STORY

MUST MEMOIRS LIE?

I closed the previous chapter by referring, once again, to the "imaginative, poetic labor of narrative" as it emerges in and through hindsight. And throughout this book, I have emphasized the idea that hindsight, rather than representing the past "as it was," reviews and reconstructs it from afar. Contra those who hold that this process cannot help but deform and falsify the past, I have suggested instead that it can be the very condition for the emergence of truth, of the sort that cannot be had in the flux of the immediate moment and that requires a measure of distance to come into being. But how far are we to take this idea of the imaginative, poetic labor of narrative? There is a very clear and obvious sense in which fictive aspects are involved in refiguring the past; even if the "audience" for the story I tell about my past is me alone, there is little doubt but that I am doing some spontaneous selecting, smoothing, and shaping. How I do so is, in part, a function of the various forms of unconsciousness considered in Chapter 5: the story I tell will always and inevitably be circumscribed by what I do not know and cannot say. On an even more basic level, though, is the magnetic pull of narrative itself, to understand, to "make sense," to find some rhyme and reason in the mystery that is my life. But what about when the story I tell is for an *actual* audience, in the form of writing, as in a memoir or autobiography? That story will not only need to make some semblance of sense to others; it will need to have some literary appeal too, and it will employ a variety of fictive devices to make that happen.

In recent years, we have seen a number of writers become quite carried away with these fictive devices. Perhaps most notorious is James Frey's *A Million Little Pieces* (2005), an Oprah Winfrey selection initially portrayed as a memoir that included elements that were eventually revealed as fictitious. As Frey himself was to admit in "a note to the reader" included in later editions of the book, "I embellished many details about my past experiences, and altered others in order to serve what I felt was the greater purpose of the book." As Frey goes on to explain, "I didn't think of what I was writing as nonfiction or fiction, memoir or autobiography." Rather, "I wanted to use my experiences to tell my story about addiction and alcoholism, about recovery, about family and friends and faith and love, about redemption and hope." He had drawn on memory as well as "supporting documents" from his journal, medical records, therapists' notes, and so on. But, by his own admission, "I wanted the stories in the book to ebb and flow, to have dramatic arcs, to have the tension that all great books require." Consequently, "I altered events and details all the way through the book." Even though, for example, he had not been directly involved in a train accident that had killed a girl from his school, his story indicated that he had. Even though he had only been in jail for several hours, the story expanded his stay into three months. In short, Frey had *lied.*

Rather than simply avowing this and calling it a day, Frey goes on to situate his process in the context of current debates about nonfiction and fiction, insisting still on using the language of "memoir," which, in his view, "allows the writer to work from memory instead of from a strict journalistic or historical standard. It is about impression and feeling, about individual recollection." In principle, there is not much to disagree with here, and many memoirists would heartily concur with this basic view. We might even buy his assessment that his book, "a combination of facts about my life and certain embellishments," reveals a "subjective truth, altered by the mind of a recovering drug addict and alcoholic." Still, with all due respect to Frey, who clearly suffered a great deal in the wake of the exposé, there is little justification in continuing to call the book a memoir and little reason to situate it in the context of current debate about the commonalities and differences between nonfiction and fiction. The fact of his having not only embellished here and there, in the name of literariness, but also blatantly lied throws the entire account into question. But what about those works that stop short of telling outright lies yet retain the fictive devices needed to have "dramatic arcs" and "the tension that all great books require"? Herein lies the dilemma: empty memoirs of such devices and they can become mere reportage or chronicles (and will likely sell many fewer copies). Include them, as virtually all memoirists do (to a greater or lesser extent), and the result cannot help but distort, even falsify, the truth of the past—or so the standard story goes. But is it so? Must memoirs lie?

REMEMBERING AND WRITING
THE PERSONAL PAST

In a provocative essay entitled "Book of Days" (2003), Emily Fox Gordon recounts the process of transforming a personal essay entitled "Mockingbird Years" into a memoir by the same title. Although she had had some misgivings about doing so—not least because she was beginning to consider the genre of memoir "problematical"—Gordon had ultimately succumbed to the idea, the result being a lucrative contract and "one of the calmest, happiest periods" of her life. "I suspected that there was something a little Faustian about the deal I made with my publisher," she admits, "but I found it difficult to fix my attention squarely on my qualms. It seemed slightly ridiculous to berate myself for accepting the terms of the marketplace and turning my essays into a memoir—a bit like putting on airs" (p. 24).

Gordon's ambivalence aside, the fact of the matter was, "*Mockingbird Years* was exactly the kind of thing a publisher loves. It was old but new, a novel variation on a familiar theme. It fit neatly into a reliably salable subcategory of the 'my story' memoir—the therapy saga—but it was distinguished from others of its kind by a contrarian twist." In Gordon's memoir, "therapy was not the vehicle of deliverance but the villain: the troubles I brought into my therapy were minor, I argued, but the destructive effects of what I called my 'therapeutic education' were not." Although she herself had read very few self-discovery memoirs, Gordon "somehow . . . had managed to absorb all the conventions of the genre. Perhaps," she muses, "it was enough just to have lived in contemporary society and to have watched TV" (p. 24). We thus return to a significant problem—should we choose to regard it as such—frequently associated with memory and narrative alike: the way we remember, and the way we tell, is suffused with conventions, with schematic, even stereotypical, renditions of the personal past, derived from count-less sources, many of which are external to our own personal experience. Psychologist Ernst Schachtel's classic essay "On

Memory and Infantile Amnesia" (in his book *Metamorphosis,* 1959) spells out this issue clearly:

> If one looks closely at the average adult's memory of the periods of his life after childhood, such memory, it is true, usually shows no great temporal gaps. It is fairly continuous. But its formal continuity in time is offset by barrenness in content, by an incapacity to reproduce anything that resembles a really rich, full, rounded, and alive experience. Even the most "exciting" events are remembered as milestones rather than as moments filled with the concrete abundance of life
>
> . . . . What is remembered is usually, more or less, only the fact that such an event took place. The signpost is remembered, not the place, the thing, the situation to which it points. And even these signposts themselves do not usually indicate the really significant moments in a person's life; rather they point to the events that are conventionally supposed to be significant, to the clichés which society has come to consider as the main stations of life. Thus the memories of the majority of people come to resemble increasingly the stereotyped answers to a question-naire, in which life consists of time and place of birth, religious denomination, residence, educational degrees, job, marriage, number and birthdates of children, income, sickness, and death. (p. 287)

As a general rule, therefore, "The processes of memory thus substitute the conventional cliché for the actual experience" (p. 291).

On some level, of course, this "substitution" is inevitable and hardly to be lamented: autobiographical memory, insofar as it makes use of language, of culturally available genres of telling, culturally sanctioned plotlines, and so on, is irrevocably bound to convention. What's more, and again, there is no question but that such memory does not, and cannot, resurrect the "actual experience"—or, as I would prefer to frame it, the "past present" experience. For the most part, that is not the purpose of auto-biographical memory; the purpose is rather to *understand*, to make sense of the past in the light of the present. Schachtel is nevertheless on to something important here, and it has to do with the simple fact that it is perilously easy to fall prey to overly schematized and conventionalized renditions of the past—ones that perhaps reveal more about extant ways of remembering and telling than about the specificities of the life in question.

In the case of those who elect to write about the past—that is, to turn their memories into narrative—the problem at hand may become that much more salient. Along these lines, Schachtel (1959) writes,

> One might well say that the greatest problem of the writer or the poet is the temptation of language. At every step a word beckons, it seems so convenient, so suitable, one has heard or read it so often in a similar context, it sounds so well, it makes the phrase flow so smoothly. If he follows the temptation of this word, he will perhaps describe something that many people recognize at once, that they already know, that follows a familiar pattern; but he will have missed the nuance that distinguishes his experience from others, that makes it his own. If he wants to communicate that elusive nuance which in some way, however small, will be his contribution, a widening or opening of the scope of articulate human experience at some point, he has to fight constantly against the easy flow of words that offer them-selves. Like the search for truth, which never reaches its goal yet never can be abandoned, the endeavor to articulate, express, and communicate an experience can never succeed completely. . . .

The lag, the discrepancy between experience and word is a productive force in man as long as he remains aware of it, as long as he knows and feels that his experience was in some way more than and different from what his concepts and words articulate. The awareness of this unexplored margin of experience, which may be its essential part, can turn into that productive energy which enables man to go one step closer to understanding and communicating his experience, and thus add to the scope of human insight. It is this awareness and the struggle and the ability to narrow the gap between experience and words which make the writer and the poet. (p. 296)

Judging from what Gordon goes on to say about *Mockingbird Years*, it is not entirely clear how successful she was in narrowing this gap. Indeed, after conducting an informal survey of self-discovery memoirs subsequent to writing her own, she reports that nearly every one—including her own—"can be reduced to the following formula":

The protagonist (1) suffers and/or is damaged, often at the hands of parents, but sometimes as the result of an illness or repressive thought system, (2) seeks out or encounters a person or institution or vocation or influence that offers escape, healing, relief from, and/or transcendence of the original suffering and/or damage. These persons or vocations or influences turn out to be false, unreliable, or inefficacious (think of drugs, gurus, false religions, sexual obsessions, bad marriages). (2) is repeated. Each time the protagonist's wish for relief is frustrated, the stakes grow higher: the reader's sympathetic identification grows and the narrative tension increases. Just at the point when the reader's pleasure threatens to become pain, the protagonist (3) stumbles across the finish line. Through the agency of yet another vocation or influence or person or institution, the protagonist at last achieves the relief, escape, or transcendence he has been seeking all along. (In my memoir, therapy was the oppressive force, writing the agent of liberation.) The drive toward narrative closure, which seems to be encrypted in human DNA, is realized in an emotionally satisfying conclusion. (pp. 24–25)

Lauren Slater, in her "metaphorical memoir" *Lying* (2000), goes one step further in her own DNA-inspired piece of psychobiological reflection on narrative when she notes that, "The neural mechanism that undergirds the lie is the same neural mechanism that helps us make narrative. Thus, all stories, even those journalists swear up and down are 'true,' are at least physiologically linked to deception" (p. 164).

That is not all. John Updike, in his book *Self-Consciousness*, notes that, "Perspectives are altered by the fact of being drawn; description solidifies the past and creates a gravitational body that wasn't there before" (1989, p. xii). Annie Dillard, reflecting on her own work, provides us with something of a warning in this context: "Don't hope in a memoir to preserve your memories because it is a certain way to lose them. . . . After you've written, you can no longer remember anything but the writing. However true you make the writing, you've created a monster. After I've written about any experience, my memories—those elusive, fragmentary patches of color and feeling—are gone. They've been replaced by the work" (1987, p. 71). For Dillard especially, there is the sense that writing about oneself, one's memories, is a kind of cat-and-mouse game: even as she tries to take hold of those "elusive, fragmentary patches," they recede and vanish. Such problems may be magnified in the case of fiction writers who decide to write their memoirs or their autobiographies. "There are some semi-fictional touches here," Mary McCarthy admits of her own *Memories of a Catholic Girlhood* (1963). "I arranged actual events so as to make a good story of them. It is hard to overcome this temptation if you are in the habit of writing fiction," McCarthy notes; "one does it almost automatically" (p. 153). Philip Roth too, in *The Facts* (1988), had to "resist the impulse to dramatize untruthfully the insufficiently dramatic, to complicate the essentially simple, to charge with implication what implied very little" (p. 7). It is perhaps with these sorts of issues in mind that all autobiography—whether carried out formally, in writing, or informally, in the context of self-interpretation—may be deemed by some to be nothing other than a species of fiction.

What much of the foregoing discussion comes down to, according to cultural historian Hayden White, is the notion that, "We do not live stories, even if we give our lives meaning by retrospectively casting them in the form of stories" (1978, p. 90). Rather, it would seem that, *really,* we just keep on, now this way, now that. What this means is that any and all stories we might tell about ourselves, particularly those we tell to others, are indeed essentially fictitious; they are vehicles for warding off the flux and for meeting our need for order—illusory though it may be to suppose that this order exists anywhere but in our own minds. Literary critic Frank Kermode (1967) gives us a somewhat subtler, less subjective perspective on much the same issue. "Men"—and women—"like poets, rush 'into the middest,' *in medias res,* when they are born; they also die *in mediis rebus,* and to make sense of their span they need fictive concords with origins and ends, such as give meaning to lives and to poems" (p. 7). But there is no small measure of deceit in this: "Novels . . . have beginnings, ends, and potentiality," Kermode goes on to say, "even if the world has not" (p. 138). Indeed, there is a distinct sense in which the novel "has to lie. Words, thought, patterns of word and thought, are enemies of truth, if you identify that with what may be had by phenomenological reductions" (p. 140). The implication? To the extent that we partake at all of these fictive strategies in the course of our own efforts at narrative reflection and writing—which on some level it would appear we must—we too must lie.

Thus far, then, three interrelated issues have surfaced that warrant our consideration as we explore the phenomenon at hand, each of them generating a paradox of sorts. The first, dealt with succinctly by Schachtel, concerns the conventional dimension of both autobiographical memory and autobiographical narrative. On the one hand, it is clear that there is no escaping this conventional dimension. It is part and parcel of our hermeneutical situation; that is, the fact that we are always already in the world—in the midst of language, culture, history (see especially Gadamer, 1975)—as we try to make sense of it. On the other hand, it is also clear that there nevertheless remains a pressure, a *narrative* pressure, to speak the truth. So it is, Schachtel told us, that the writer must always strive to move beyond convention—or, perhaps more appropriately put, to imaginatively *rework* convention in such a way that something new can be said.

The second issue concerns the sources of memory and narrative. Gordon told us that perhaps she had learned some elements of the genre of memoir simply by living in contemporary society and watching TV (and seeing movies, reading books, going to the theater, and so on). What she has also told us, in effect (confirming a point discussed in Chapter 4), is that these external sources have in fact become internalized and that the resultant narrative—as well as the memory on which it relies—is a curious admixture of her own "firsthand" experiences and those "secondhand" experiences bequeathed from without. Something of a paradox thus exists here too, and it is not unrelated to the first one we encountered: just as there is no extricating memory and narrative from convention, there is no extricating that which is wholly "ours" from that which derives from without. The tendency is to reserve the term "memory" for the former, the supposition being that knowledge derived from external (secondhand) sources gets imposed on the internal (firsthand) material. But if these external sources become constitutive of the very fabric of our minds, including our memories, how are we ever to separate out internal from external, the "actual" from the "imposed"? And yet: there is a pressure here too, to do precisely this, a pressure to rely on *our own* memories and to tell *our own* stories as best we can. What can this possibly mean?

The third issue is more vexing still. While Gordon had spoken of an inherent drive toward narrative closure,[1] Slater and Kermode had gone so far as to relate the process of narrating to *lying*. They are not alone in this. "Autobiography is hopelessly inventive," cognitive psychologist Michael Gazzaniga (1998) insists. A "special device" in the brain he calls the *interpreter* "reconstructs . . . brain events and in doing so makes telling errors of perception, memory, and judgment" (p. 2). The interpreter also tries "to keep our personal story together." And, "To do that, we have to learn to lie to ourselves. . . . We need something that expands the actual facts of our experience into an ongoing narrative, the self-image we have been building in our mind for years. The spin doctoring that goes on keeps us

---

[1] See also Kermode's (1978) notion that, as readers, we are all "pleromatists," seeking the "center" that would allow interpretation to cease; also Smith's (1988) notion of "claustrophilia."

believing that we are good people, that we are in control and mean to do good. It is probably the most amazing mechanism the human being possesses" (pp. 26–27). The interpreter, therefore, "tells us the lies we need to believe in order to remain in control" (p. 138). Add writing to this spin doctoring process—writing that may well be oriented toward convincing others that we are good people too—and the lies become that much more pronounced. Is there a way beyond these paradoxes?

"Big Stories"

Let us return to Gordon's essay to flesh out these difficult issues further. "When I think of *Mockingbird Years,*" she writes,

> I picture it as a crude map depicting the three essays from which it originated as aboriginal landmasses. In my mind, they are connected by a series of narrative bridges, long chains of interlocking "and then, and then, and then(s)." Even though I had adapted the original essays for use in the memoir, I view them as uncontestable territories—pieces of the truth. The narrative bridges, on the other hand, seem to me to be flimsy things, instrumentally constructed, spanning a watery chaos. (p. 25)

Gordon acknowledges that the essays she had written were also constructions, as much as the narrative parts that would eventually unite them. She also acknowledges that the essays themselves partake of elements of narrative and that, consequently, they are hardly to be regarded as pure, immune from the sort of "flimsiness" she has come to associate with the narrative bridges. As such, she writes, "I find it hard to account for my settled conviction that they were somehow *truer* than the parts I viewed as narrative bridges" (p. 25). But the conviction was there, along with an "uneasy conscience." Something was amiss at the very heart of the memoir—indeed, perhaps at the very heart of *memory* itself.

"As memoirs go," Gordon notes, "mine is fairly honest." She does "take a few liberties here and there with details of décor and landscape," but unlike Frey and company, "there are no large-scale inventions, no outright untruths." Moreover, "Everything that I say happened in my memoir happened, and happened more or less when I said it did." What, then, is the problem? In what sense had she "distorted the truth of [her] life almost beyond recognition?" (p. 26). Here is her answer, which she frames in terms of "the tripartite lie of contemporary memoir":

> First, I presented what was only one of a multitude of possible autobiographical stories as if it were the story of my life. . . . Next, I allowed this narrative to influence the selections I made from the nearly infinite set of possibilities—and orderings of possibilities—that my life history afforded me. . . . Finally, and most seriously, I wrote from an impossibly posthumous point of view, as if I knew the final truth of my life—as if I were confident that nothing that happened in the future might yet revise it. While I was careful to hedge my bet with irony and a certain tentativeness of tone, I knew in my writer's heart that where I left off, my readers would take over—their passion for narrative closure would finish the job for me. And then they would hoist me onto their shoulders and make much of me, or at least some of them would. The odd consequence of the lie of my memoir was that my mere, and logically necessary, survival was enough to turn my story into a triumph. (p. 26)

Through hindsight—through what felt like the wisdom of hindsight—there had emerged a storyline that would codify, and solidify, the past, the seemingly inevitable result being a multidimensional lie.

"The difficulty is insurmountable," Georges Gusdorf (1980) has written: "no trick of presentation even when assisted by genius can prevent the narrator from always knowing the outcome of the story he tells—he commences, in a manner of speaking, with the problem already solved." Moreover, in line with what Gordon has told us, "the illusion begins from the moment that the narrative *confers a meaning* on the event which, when it actually occurred, no doubt had several meanings or perhaps none. This postulating of a meaning dictates the choice of the facts to be retained and of the details to bring out or to dismiss according to the demands of the preconceived intelligibility." According to Gusdorf, "It is here that the failures, the gaps, and the deformations of memory find their origin; they are not due to purely physical cause nor to chance, but on the contrary they are the result of an option of the writer who remembers and wants to gain acceptance for this or that revised and corrected version of his past, his private reality" (p. 42). Thus, for Gordon and Gusdorf alike, the problem is not only knowing the ending, thus limiting the multitude of possible stories to be told and allowing the resultant narrative scheme to determine what is to be included and excluded; there is also the problem of readership: the act of writing, they have suggested, cannot be separated from the writer's wishes, conscious or unconscious, for affirmation and applause.

Bearing the issue of readership in mind, there is also the problem of narrative itself. Gordon's perspective is a curious one. "I feel a little ashamed that I was so ready to sell my essayistic birthright for a mess of memoiristic pottage," she confesses, "but I can't deny that my book was better, or at least more readable, for having a story line. A narrative arc is necessary to a memoir of the kind I contracted to write, particularly one that encompasses all or most of a life and brings it up to the present day." Her explanation: "It's the length that does it: the brain will submit to an amoebically free-form twenty-page essay, but will balk at the prospect of three hundred pages without a through-line" (p. 27). The intra-psychic lie that Gazzaniga had spoken of, which was needed "to keep our personal story together," is thus magnified in the case of memoir; without it, Gordon implies, readers' brains would simply tune out after twenty pages and sales would plummet. This, at least, is how it all appears now.

"For two years after *Mockingbird Years* was published," Gordon continues,

> I struggled to disentangle the triumphant narrative self of my memoir from my necessarily non-triumphant real self. I lost touch with my real past, and consequently lost access to the future; I was unable to live and consequently unable to write. Like a character under a fairy-tale curse, I had no choice but to wait until a sense of the actual past returned to me—until the season of my false triumph had passed and the weeds of authenticity had grown high enough to obscure the orderly garden of memoir. (p. 27)

Fair enough: clearly, a significant gap had opened between the story Gordon had told and who she really believed herself to be. But is the problem here the seeming inevitability of hindsight and narrative working their self-aggrandizing ways? Or is it that Gordon had written an overly self-aggrandizing narrative, one that simply wasn't as truthful as it might have been? *Must* autobiographical narrative be triumphalist? *Must* the "garden" of memoir be as orderly as she suggests? Again, *must* memoir lie?

My colleague and friend Michael Bamberg and I have had a spirited debate in recent years about the virtues of "small" versus "big" stories.[2] From his perspective, the sorts of big-story narratives found in memoirs and other "life story" forms are suspect by virtue of their distance from the experiences they seek to depict, their seemingly inevitable recourse to speculative conjecture, and, not least, their very "size"—which, he has suggested (not unlike Gordon), requires just that sort of narrative "through-line" that cannot help but take us away from the actualities of the past. For Gordon, a twenty-page piece of work, however "amoebically free-form" it may be, is fine; the brain can handle it. For Bamberg, similarly, small stories are the way to go—if, that is, the aim is to be faithful to the promised land of "real life." As for the rather bigger stories I tend to explore, he adds, they are best understood as embodying life "on holiday," the product of just that sort of reflective pause that is intrinsic to hindsight and narrative reflection alike. Bamberg acknowledges that big stories do seem to make for better reading. But their very distance from the experiential thick of things—from the scenarios that surge in and out of life, in conversation, in action, in just being in the world—cast their value into question. If there are to be any narratives at all, therefore, they are going to have to be quite small.

LIFE BEFORE NARRATIVE?

The plot thickens. "The past I longed to retrieve was not just the past unmediated by the story of a life in therapy, but the past unmediated by any narrative at all. I wanted to rediscover my

---

[2] See Bamberg, 2006; Freeman, 2006; also Georgakopoulou, 2006 for an instance of this exchange.

history under the aspect of nothing but itself." Gordon, therefore, essentially wanted to engage in a kind of time travel, to a land before narrative, to a past whose future was as yet undetermined. "How did this past look as I turned back to face it? Very much the way the future looked to me as a child—like a great undifferentiated ocean of time. Here and there, events and impressions heaved up to break the surface of the unmapped waters of the past, but I had very little sense of the geography of the region" (p. 27). Fortunately, there had been lots of baby pictures of her daughter, which Gordon would be able to explore "as hungrily as an archeologist examining the artifacts of a lost civilization." She needed these pictures; "without them I could no longer bring to mind the stages of a face that changed every week. How much more of the lost world of my history might I have been able to reclaim if I had taken more pictures, kept other kinds of records of time as it was passing?" Not only did these photos help Gordon remember her daughter as she had appeared throughout the course of her childhood; they also gave her "a foothold in time. Having recovered [her daughter's] red denim overalls," for instance, "I can also retrieve other details and scenes through association, and thus triangulate my way back into an era of which they have come to be an emblem. Those photographs— or at least a few of them—have become the central nodes of a whole system of recollection" (p. 28).

Gordon is hardly to be faulted for wanting to return to those earlier days via the baby pictures; they allow a different kind of relationship to the past, one that is more concrete, more sensuous. But it is unclear why this relationship ought to be elevated to the status of Truth and memoir demoted to that of the lie. A twofold assumption is operative in Gordon's essay as well as in the work of many theorists of autobiographical memory and narrative. The first part of the assumption is that immediate experience—that which occurs in the context of the sensuous present moment—is taken to be a kind of baseline of the Real; it is the foundation against which all other accounts are to be compared, the indubitable archive of What Really Happened. The second part follows from the first: insofar as memory—and, by extension, narrative—veer away from the fleshy immediacy of the (past) present moment, they cannot help but involve some measure of distortion. Oftentimes, following Sir Frederic Bartlett's line of thinking (1995 [1932]) especially, theorists use the more neutral language of "reconstruction." For instance, Daniel Schacter's edited volume *Memory Distortion* (1995) is subtitled *How Minds, Brains, and Societies Reconstruct the Past.* But there is no mistaking the thrust of the work, its most fundamental question being: "Under what conditions is memory largely accurate, and under what conditions is distortion most likely to occur?" (p. 25). The leading terms are "accuracy" and "distortion," "true" memories, which correspond to reality, and "false" ones, which deform it. The implication is clear enough: to the degree that memory departs from What Really Happened, in the sensuous fullness of immediate experience, it cannot help but falsify the past. As noted earlier, sometimes this process may be quite useful; distortion can serve to cover over realities we might wish to forget, or bolster our self-esteem, or provide for us the comforting illusion that our lives have an immanent order, meaning, or purpose. But it is no less fictive—in the sense of false—for all that. Add writing to the mix, and the problems are redoubled, for what we have, it would seem, is a reconstruction of a reconstruction—indeed, a fiction of a fiction—the very attempt to convey in words the shifting sands of memorial meaning adding another layer of separation from the Real.

I want to question this twofold assumption. First, I question the tendency to equate the immediate, the momentary, the sensuous present, with "reality." It is *one* reality, to be sure, but there is no necessary reason to consider it primary—the "baseline"against which any and all other renditions are to be compared. Indeed, as we have seen, there are profound *limits* to the present moment, because of our all-too-human tendency to be unreflectively caught up in it and because we do not yet know the role it will play in the evolving stories of our lives. Please understand: I do not wish to denigrate the present moment! Following psychiatrist Daniel Stern especially (see his *The Present Moment in Psychotherapy and Everyday Life* [2004]), it surely has virtues of its own. What's more, it can certainly be argued, compellingly, that too often we are *blind* to the present moment, moving through our lives all too hastily, all too unaware of what's *there*, before us, in the world. As noted earlier, the recent work of Eckhart Tolle (e.g., 2004) is relevant here, not to mention the rich traditions of Eastern thought from which it derives. There are nevertheless limits to the present moment, tied not only to blindness, hastiness, lack of awareness, and so on, but also, as I have suggested throughout this book, to the absence of that sort of temporal distance that allows us to see things in their full, or at least fuller, measure. As Gadamer (1975) puts the matter, "what a thing has to say, its intrinsic content, first appears only after it is divorced from the fleeting circumstances of its actuality" (p. 265). As such, temporal distance, so often assumed to be a source of distortion or outright falsification, bears within it a "positive and productive possibility of understanding" (p. 264).

I also question what might be termed the "reconstructive-memory-as-inevitable-distortion" thesis. Let me be clear about this too: there *can* be hindsight bias, there *can* be false memories, and all the rest. Inquiring into these sorts of issues is vitally important. This focus on accuracy and distortion, however, is only one axis of inquiry into the reconstructive dimension of hindsight and of memory more generally. As such, I want to turn to a quite different axis of inquiry, my primary interest being in the *revelatory* power of hindsight—that is, its capacity to yield insight and understanding, indeed *truth,* of a sort that *cannot* occur in the immediacy of the present moment.

Gordon herself has clearly made use of this revelatory power. As she now realizes,

> The narrative of my memoir was a lie, and for some time it made my entire history disappear. . . . Like every story, it was told after the fact. I had no way of knowing until quite late that I would hear any call [to become a writer] at all, and when I did, I seized upon it to justify what was failed in my life. My memory subsequently colluded with the narrative scheme by consigning everything unrelated or potentially antagonistic to it—my studies; my motherhood; my marriage; the pleasures, pains, and struggles of my daily life; the ambition that I could hardly contain, much less conceal from myself; even the writing I did before I pronounced myself a writer—to relative obscurity, so as to dramatize my modest success by throwing it into bold relief. (p. 30)

There is a tragic aspect to this new story Gordon wishes to tell about herself. "The only way I seem to be able to reclaim my own experience," she writes, "is to remember it 'under the aspect'—under the aspect, that is, of narrative interpretation, which initiates distortions of the past as automatically as a rent in a stocking begins a run. . . . What comes later in a life draws its significance from what came earlier, but only in the dead letter of a narrative can what comes earlier draw its significance from what comes later. Life can be read backward, not forward" (p. 30).

Where does this leave her? "My long-odds bet [about becoming a writer] paid off," Gordon writes, "but even so, my reckless dismissal of so much in my life that did not fit my notion of destiny is something to regret." Then a brief meditation on this idea: "Regret. What can I make of this anachronistic sentiment? Regret is the obverse of the triumphalism I've been describing here. Its voice is quiet; in a noisily therapeutic age, all but inaudible" (pp. 30–31). But there is an ironic twist to this final rendition of things: the very insight that Gordon has attained—about herself, about the seemingly inevitable distortions of the past, about the lie of memoir—*has itself derived from hindsight,* as has her regret. And yet, it is precisely this measure of insight—attainable *only* in hindsight, via narrative reflection—that is belied by the insistence on the lie of memoir and of narrative interpretation more generally.

RECLAIMING THE REAL, RETHINKING THE TRUE

Let me conclude this chapter with several fairly strong assertions about the relationship between "fiction" and "reality" as these terms apply to autobiographical narratives. The first is that the notion of *fiction,* when used to refer to the processes that go into the fashioning of life narratives, is too often parasitic on an overly narrow—and very problematic—notion of what reality is; and as a consequence, it ends up being degraded, given a lesser status. The second assertion is that this conception of reality is problematic because it is equated with the allegedly raw and pristine, the uninterpreted and unconstructed, and because it is tied to a conception of time—basically, clock time, the time of lines, instants, sequences—that is better applied to the world of *things* than to the world of *people.* Thus, the conception of reality that usually surfaces when memoirs and autobiographies are relegated to the status of fictions—or *mere* fictions, as they are often called—is one that is imagined to somehow be free of our own designs, a string of "stuff" that just happens, in time, and that we will inevitably falsify when we later look backward and try to impose some order. This conception simply does not do justice to the dynamic complexity of temporal experience. The third idea is that, by rethinking the notion of the fictive, there is the possibility not only of "reclaiming" the real—by which I mean restoring to it a fuller and more comprehensive range of meanings—but also of establishing a more adequate rendition of what *truth* might mean in the human realm.

Occasionally, our memories can in fact lead us back to something like, or something that *feels* like, the past; that is, a previously present experience, a reliving. Gordon's photos seemed to be able to bring her to such a place. More often, however, particularly when we are trying to make sense not just of an event but of some significant period of the personal past— some chapter, as it were—we don't at all seek to "recapture" what was, in its openness and indeterminacy. Rather, we interpret the past from the standpoint of the present, seeking to determine how it might have contributed to this very moment; and this is a determination that cannot possibly be made until this moment has arrived. The present must therefore await the future in order for larger orders of meaning and significance to be discerned. This discernment can only happen in hindsight, via narrative reflection. As the philosopher David Carr (1986) has succinctly put the matter, "Narrative requires narration," and narration has at its core a dimension of distance. "What is essential to the story-teller's position," therefore, "is the advantage of . . . hindsight," which bears within it a "freedom from the constraint of the present assured by occupying a position after, above, or outside the events narrated" (p. 60).

The philosopher Ian Hacking's (1995) work may be helpful here as well. He reflects on the indeterminacy not of memory, but of the *past*, "the indeterminacy of what people actually did" (p. 235). The idea isn't that we simply find out more about the past (although, clearly, that sometimes happens); it is that "we present actions under new descriptions" (p. 243). As Hacking goes on to note, "What matters to us may not have been quite so definite as it now seems. When we remember what we did, or what other people did, we may also rethink, redescribe, and refeel the past. These redescriptions," he writes, "may be perfectly true of the past. That is, they are truths that we now assert about the past. And yet, paradoxically, they may not have been true in the past" (p. 249). Notice in this context that, although these truths emerge in and through narrative reflection, from looking backward over the landscape of the past from the vantage point of the present, Hacking speaks not of *narrative truth,* which is frequently cast in more "subjective" terms, but simply of *truth.*[3] He is thus encouraging us to expand our sense of what truth might be by taking it beyond that which represents the discrete events of the past. What is being considered here is a truth that is *made available* in hindsight, via narrative reflection.

Indeed, as I have suggested elsewhere (Freeman, 2003b), the narrated life is the examined life, where one steps out from the flow of things and seeks to become more conscious of one's existence. Along these lines, autobiographical narratives are not only about what happened when, how these happenings might

---

[3] Psychoanalyst Donald Spence's *Narrative Truth and Historical Truth* (1982) remains the best-known example of the two-truths idea. See also Ludwig, 1997. For a critique, see Freeman, 1985, 2002b.

be emplotted, and so forth, but also about how to live, and whether the life is a good one. The pressure that may be felt toward telling the truth of one's life, impossible though it may seem upon an initial glance, is therefore partly cognitive and partly ethical. The classical notion of recollection, or *anamnesis,* is very much about this dual demand. On the one hand, there is reference to recounting and understanding. But there is also a reference to "gathering together," to remembering what is most significant and worthwhile in a sometimes forgetful life. This dual demand can be brought to fulfillment in and through hindsight. I shall return to this theme in the chapter to come.

To the extent that one equates "reality" with immediate experience, autobiographical recollections are bound to be seen as distortions, even falsifications. And if truth is understood to be that which "imitates" this reality, then autobiographical narratives, in turn, are bound to be seen as fictions. Finally, if both reality and truth are predicated in terms of linear, or clock, time—this happened, this happened, this happened, our experiences simply ticking away, one after the other—then the entire autobiographical enterprise becomes condemned to the status of being "hopelessly inventive," as Gazzaniga had put it: because there is no possibility of ever returning to those ticking moments and telling it like it really was, autobiography—and, by extension, the process of narrative reflection—can lead to nothing but illusions. From this quite strange perspective, it would seem that we are born liars, and it is the very existence of self-consciousness that seems to be at fault.

But there is a conflation here: *narrativity,* by virtue of its constructiveness, is being linked with *fictionality,* such that the constructed becomes the *untrue.* What's more, the very process of *interpretation* itself becomes, from this perspective, suspect as a vehicle of understanding. Both of these suppositions, however, ultimately rely on a kind of covert positivism, one that presumes, paradoxically, that the only true view is the proverbial view from nowhere. "Choosing, selecting, and simplifying do not amount to falsifying what is before us," Alexander Nehamas (1985) has insisted in his study on Nietzsche, "unless we believe that there can be a representation of the world that depends on no selection at all, and that this representation represents the standard of accuracy" (p. 56). Nehamas also considers the problem of assuming interpretation to be "mere," which, in effect, presupposes "that to consider a view an interpretation is to concede that it is false" (p. 66). What I am suggesting here, along with Nehamas, is the need to think beyond this perspective. And the key to doing this, I believe, lies in moving beyond clock time and seeing in *narrative time* (see Chapter 3) a possible inroad into rethinking the idea of truth.

Recollection, Paul Ricoeur (1981b) has suggested, inverts the ostensibly "natural" order of time: "by reading the end in the beginning and the beginning in the end, we learn also to read time itself backward, as the recapitulating of the initial conditions of a course of action in its terminal consequences" (p. 176). "Ordinary time," he goes on to explain (1988), "can be characterized as a series of point-like 'nows,' whose intervals are measured by our clocks. Defined in this way, time deserves to be called 'now time'" (p. 86). I have referred to this as "clock time," and there is no questioning its place in our lives. "The only thing unacceptable," Ricoeur quickly adds, "is the claim that this representation be held to be the true concept of time" (p. 87). It is but one concept of time, and it does well to organize and order those features of the world characterized by linearity, by the inexorable forwardness of (certain) natural processes. But it cannot and does not do justice to those features of the human realm that go beyond linearity, that involve movement not only from past to present but from present to past, ever again.

This movement, as Ricoeur suggests, is most visible in recollection, in that sort of explicit gathering-together that emerges in and through hindsight. But it is also part and parcel of experience itself. On one level, Hayden White (1978) and others are quite right to say that we do not live stories—at least not of the sort that we might explicitly write, when we "take the time" to take stock of our lives. As philosopher Anthony Paul Kerby (1991) acknowledges, "we are not self-consciously narrating ourselves all the time" (p. 8). Nevertheless, he quickly adds, "we are always already caught up in narratives," such that "the implicit narrative structure of life is taken up and augmented in our explicit narratives" (p. 12). So it is that Kerby speaks of the "quasi-narrative" nature of experience and Ricoeur (1991) of its "pre-narrative" nature, as well as the idea of "life as a story in its nascent state . . . an *activity and a passion in search of a narrative.*" Ricoeur thus wishes "to grant to experience as such a virtual narrativity which stems, not from the projection of literature onto life, but which constitutes a genuine demand for narrative" (p. 29). Indeed: "Without leaving the sphere of everyday experience, are we not inclined to see in a given chain of episodes in our own life something like *stories that have not yet been told,* stories that demand to be told, stories that offer points of anchorage for the narrative?" (p. 30). We are "entangled" in stories, Ricoeur reminds us; narrating is a secondary process "grafted" onto this entanglement. "Recounting, following, understanding stories is then simply the continuation of these unspoken stories" (p. 30).

None of what is being said here, again, removes the fact that we *do* sometimes project meanings onto the past, that we do sometimes fictionalize it, and that we do sometimes mistake illusory convictions for insights. Hence, something that initially appears to be in the service of self-understanding may in fact not be; it may instead be in the service of defense, self-protection. Consider the poisoned rendition of the past we encountered in Chapter 5 through the story of Samuel. Consider more generally the fact that some people have images of their past and of themselves that are patently false, that fly in the face of what virtually everyone else sees and knows: her life was not the ceaseless string of traumas she made it out to be; his life was not the romantic odyssey he had always said it was but something else, something bleaker and darker. As philosopher Owen Flanagan (1996) has noted, some people do indeed succumb to "a deeply fictional and far-fetched account of the self," such that "the self projected for both public and first-person consumption may be strangely and transparently out of kilter with what the agent is like." This sort of "misguided self-representation," Flanagan adds, is constitutive of "the misguided person's actual full identity" (p. 69). But it is no less misguided—and *false*—for all that.

However skittish we may be about embracing ideas like truth at this particular juncture in history, few, I would venture, would dispute the distinct possibility that we can fall prey to illusion and self-deception, to spinning fictions and fantasies about who and what we are. But this idea of self-deception makes no sense apart from some conception of what it might mean to be *non*-deceived. One of the great challenges of autobiographical understanding and writing, therefore, has to do with the capacity to *resist* such fictions and fantasies, at least those that are illusory or harmful, and to move in the direction of truth. In speaking of truth in this manner, however, it should be emphasized that we have moved far from the customary way of conceiving it, that is, in terms of discrete propositions that somehow correspond to the reality of the past. We have also moved far from thinking of it as some sort of fictive imposition onto the past that inevitably falsifies it. The truth of the past—indeed, the truth of a *life*—is neither strictly "found" nor strictly "made." Instead, it is aptly considered as a kind of "region," a psychic space that becomes inhabitable. But what exactly does this mean, and how does one come to live there?

I have come to find the idea of *poiesis* particularly valuable in this context.[4] As a general rule, the poet is in the business neither of finding meanings, already there in the world, nor of making them, in the sense of fashioning them wholly anew. Rather, the poet is engaged in a process in which meaning is at once found *and* made—or, to be more explicit still, in which *meaning is found through being made.* When referring to poiesis as meaning-making, therefore, the intent is to highlight the constructive, imaginative dimension of the process of articulating and understanding the world, both inner and outer. But this very dimension, it must be emphasized, is ultimately in the service of disclosing—"unconcealing," as Heidegger (1971) might put it—the reality of the past. Only through the creative labor of the poet does there exist the possibility of disclosing what is there, in the world. And only through the creative labor of the narrative imagination does there exist the possibility of disclosing the meaning and significance of times past.

Contra those who believe narrative understanding entails the inevitable falsification of the past or fictionalization of the self, I suggest that it is better seen as the very condition of their existence: the past *qua* past, along with the self whose past it is, issue from the imaginative labor that is part and parcel of narrative reflection. "Our life, when then embraced in a single glance, appears to us as the field of a constructive

---

[4] See Freeman, 1999, 2002b, 2002c; see also Chapter 2.

activity, borrowed from narrative understanding, by which we attempt to discover and not simply to impose from outside the *narrative identity which constitutes us*" (Ricoeur, 1991, p. 32). Ricoeur does well in this piece to spell out the interrelationship between the narrativity that is part and parcel of life itself, the actual narratives we tell about our lives, and the narrative identity that grows out of the two. What he is therefore suggesting, implicitly at any rate, is that human lives themselves may profitably be understood as a kind of *literature*— different from those more highly organized forms found on bookshelves and the like but literary in their essence. This way of framing things may well have provided a measure of solace to Gordon. Perhaps life and narrative are not so far apart as she had assumed. Perhaps hindsight can be a source not only of error but of insight, even wisdom. And perhaps there is a deeper, more capacious way of thinking about truth than the way she had.

" 'Truth,' " Nietzsche (1968 [1888]) writes, is not something "there" to be found, like an inert thing, "but something that must be created and that gives a name to a process, or rather to a will to overcome that has in itself no end—introducing truth as a *processus in infinitum,* an active determining—not a becoming conscious of something that is in itself firm and determined" (p. 552). As the philosopher Wilhelm Dilthey (1976 [1910]) adds, referring explicitly to autobiographical understanding, "Between the parts we see a connection which neither is, nor is intended to be, the simple likeness of a life of so many years, but which, because understanding is involved, expresses what the individual knows about the continuity of his life" (p. 215). Along these lines, the truth of a life, and the "narrative connectedness" from which it may emerge, is a function of "active authorial work on the agent's part" (Flanagan, 1996, p. 66), the building of just those sorts of narrative bridges that Gordon had found so "flimsy." But it is also a function of a kind of *listening*, we might say, one that takes time off from "working" and attends to the past openly and open-mindedly.[5] Patricia Hampl (1999) puts the matter well: "Intimacy with a piece of writing, as with a person, comes from paying attention to the revelations it is capable of giving, not by imposing my own notions and agenda, no matter how well intentioned they might be" (p. 28). The situation is much the same in the case of narrative reflection: it derives instead from attending carefully, and imaginatively, to the movement of the past. In terms of writing about the past, it is also about attention to language, about the possibility of arriving at words that will somehow be able to articulate, and do justice to, the phenomena being considered.

Returning to Schachtel (1959), the task of the writer is to "fight constantly against the easy flow of words that offer themselves" (p. 296) in order to find those that will say something new and valuable, something that moves beyond the cliché, the stale sentiment, into a region of truth. Finally, then, autobiographical poiesis, of the sort we find both in narrative reflection and in the stories we consciously craft in writing, is about the challenge of disclosing the truth through the difficult, never-ending process of fashioning language that is adequate both to the past and the present we seek to understand. This truth is one that can only be disclosed via the unique form of poiesis found in narrative. And far from being of a lesser kind, it is, I suggest, fundamental for the distinctive mode of being in the world we call "human."

---

[5] See especially Jonathan Lear's (1998) *Open-Minded: Working Out the Logic of the Soul.*

SEVEN

THE GOOD LIFE

TRUTH AND GOODNESS

There is more to Emily Fox Gordon's story than what I have addressed thus far. Toward the end of her (2003) essay, for instance, she recalls it having occurred to her "that there was something to be said for planning to make a life instead of planning to make a story of my life." Perhaps this gets closer to the heart of the matter. Perhaps her guilt and regret were a function not only of the *kind* of story she was eventually to tell, which she couldn't help but see as an outright lie, but of the very project of storytelling. Why couldn't she just *live?* "How many times have I comforted myself with the old saw about how the unexamined life is not worth living?" In her case, however, it had come to feel that "the reverse might well be truer—that the unlived life might not be worth examining" (p. 31). For Gordon, it almost seems as if the relationship between living and telling could be formulated as a zero-sum game: had she lived more, she might have told less. There also might have been fewer glaring discrepancies between what was and how she came to tell about it. But it could be that living and telling are not so far apart as she implies. And it could also be that the process of telling stories, rather than leading straightaway to lies, can lead in the direction of truth. That, at least, is the story I tried to tell in the previous chapter.

I do not wish to be overly objectivistic in framing the issues this way. Discerning the truth via narrative reflection is inevitably a function of the interpretive prejudices one brings to the task and is a highly contestable process. It is also an essentially open process, subject to revision. The truth disclosed in some given act of narrative reflection cannot be neatly encapsulated, contained, and may well be superseded in the future, by another, and another again. It is precisely for these reasons that I spoke in the previous chapter of a *region* of truth rather than a discretely bounded one. It is not to be "had," grasped, like some obdurate thing, unchanged, evermore. It is rather to be inhabited, as I had put it, by degrees. There is insight, enlightenment, the development of understanding; what had heretofore been misguided, obscure, or opaque becomes clearer.

But there is more, still, to be gleaned from Gordon's account of things. For, judging by the words just quoted, what she ultimately is trying to come to terms with in this essay is not only the truth but also the *goodness* of her very life. This has been so, to a greater or lesser extent, for all of the lives that have been explored here, including my own. Looking back on the ride home with my father, I took great pleasure in the fact that he and I had finally been able to "meet," to connect with one another. There is no question but that my life had become better for it: communication, connection, and the expression of love brought me closer to him as well as to an ideal. In Primo Levi's case, the situation was of course decidedly more tragic. Upon liberation from the chaotic animality of concentration camp life, he could see—or believed he could see—this animality in himself. As Levi's story shows, telling the story of the past can be perilous indeed: having been caught up in the moment, the story he tells is suffused with shame and was destined to remain so. In his own eyes, he had fallen short; he had lived a life that was less than fully human. This realization, in its very negativity, itself bespeaks a more ideal mode and is thus testimony to the magnitude of Levi's virtue. Would that he could have received some solace from it. Consider as well the brief story of my identity-expanding encounter with Berlin and Eva Hoffman's discovery of the depths of her own identity as a member of the second generation. In both of these cases, albeit in quite different ways, a connection had been formed to a sphere of life heretofore unseen and unknown. Coming to consciousness about this connection was itself a movement in the direction of a deeper, more fully examined life. As for the two artists we encountered in Chapter 5, it is clear that the process of narrative reflection had occasioned some intensive taking-stock not only of their art but also of their lives. While the result for Samuel would be the pain of failing to measure up to the greats and to live their sacred stories, for Leah, it would be the joy of finding her way, finally, after having been seduced by images and unspoken rules about what to do and who to be. In this last case, as in several of the others, there is a sense in which the insights attained are acts of *destruction*: of one's previous understandings of things and of the self whose understandings they were. The flip side of this destruction, however, is *creation*—of a more adequate, enlightened view and of a self that has moved one step further in the direction of good.

We encountered the moral dimension of narrative in particu-larly acute form in considering Levi. It was there, in Chapter 3, that I spoke of moral lateness and the horror of its realization in hindsight: by virtue especially of our pervasive tendency to get caught up in the moment, our understanding of this or that experience is delayed, put on hold, until some time in the future, when we can look backward and see what has gone on. So it is that hindsight may provide a corrective lens for the shortsighted-ness of the immediate moment and hence a vehicle for moral discernment and growth. But the corrective work of hindsight goes significantly beyond the terrain of moments, discrete occa-sions. As we have begun to see already, particularly via Gordon, it can apply to the whole of the life one has lived. Indeed, I suggest that narrative reflection, insofar as it is focused on "my life" as a whole, cannot help but be oriented toward the moral dimension. By "moral," you may recall, I refer not only to those specific spheres of experience associated with "good" and "bad" behavior (i.e. , to "morality") but also to those broader spheres of experi-ence, frequently subsumed under the rubric of "ethics," having to do with the goodness of our very lives.

Not unlike "truth," "goodness" is a term that can make many a modern mind squirm. For some, it connotes a kind of singu-larity, even absoluteness. Questions abound: *Whose* good? Who gets to define it? What is it? These are important questions. But there is no getting around the fact that, when I pause to reflect on my life, I do so, as a matter of course and necessity, against the backdrop of the question of goodness. Charles Taylor's discussion of "frameworks" in his monumental *Sources of the Self: The Making of Modern Identity* (1989) is particularly useful in this context. "To articulate a framework," he writes, "is to explicate what makes sense of our moral responses" (p. 26). It is a structure of hierarchically ordered commitments, an identifi-cation of one's priorities. It is true these frameworks have less "ontological solidity" than those that have existed in times past; identifying one's priorities is frequently difficult and precarious, permeated by uncertainty and doubt. But "doing without these frameworks is utterly impossible for us; otherwise put, that the horizons within which we live our lives and which make sense of them have to include these strong qualitative discriminations" (p. 27). More to the point still, "we cannot do without some orientation to the good" (p. 33). Indeed, "we are only selves insofar as we move in a certain space of questions, as we seek and find an orientation to the good" (p. 34). This is precisely where narrative enters the picture: "This sense of the good," Taylor insists, "has to be woven into my life as an unfolding story. . . . Making sense of my present action, when we are not dealing with such trivial questions as where I shall go in the next five minutes but with the issue of my place relative to the good, requires a narrative understanding of my life, a sense of what I have become which can only be given in a story." What's more, "as I project my life forward and endorse the existing direction or give it a new one, I project a future story, not just a state of the momentary future but a bent for my whole life to come" (p. 48).

Taylor is not particularly interested in specifying *the* nature of goodness here; in accordance with the aforementioned lessening of the "ontological solidity" of our frameworks for living, he acknowledges the "diverse aspirations" that individuals have. But if he is right, these aspirations are "ineradicable" features of human life. So too is the two-way temporal traffic that characterizes reflection on our lives: narrative understanding moves backward, into the past, and projects itself forward, into the future, providing the contours of my story-to-be.[1] Through "big story" narrative reflection of the sort being considered here, therefore—that is, reflection on the meaning and movement of my life as a whole—I orient myself, inescapably, toward the question of the good. This does not necessarily mean, of

---

[1] See also Freeman, 1984; MacIntyre, 1981.

course, that I will bask in the glow of the goodness in question. As I look back on my life, I may see little more than missed opportunities and moral wreckage. But this seeing—this very identification of the *not*-good—can only issue from some sense, however indefinite and ill-formed, of the very goodness my life has failed to be. Not unlike what was said about truth, it may be said that goodness too exists in a kind of region, an open space that one inhabits by degrees.

In some instances, such as Primo Levi's, it may feel impossible to move fully into this region. Instead, one may feel locked in the purgatory of the not-good, encased in shame and regret. Goodness here is simultaneously ubiquitous and absent, its weight being manifested only as negation. This is another way of speaking about narrative foreclosure: no projection into the future is possible, for the future has been sealed shut. Nor, in turn, can there be movement in the direction of the good. One can only move backward, under its shadow. It might be noted that, in extreme cases, the not-good may not be accompanied by any intimations of the good at all. Logically, the two are inseparable, but not psychologically: at the level of felt experience, there may be little more than the void of negativity, the not, the no, the never. This is the ultimate sphere of foreclosure, and, for some, suicide may serve as the only possible ending.

In other instances—at the next "stage," as it were, of movement in the direction of the good—one may find, in the recognition of the not-good, an intimation of a better way, but be unable to articulate this way, to specify and name it. This can result in a kind of existential frustration, for despite having identified the "bad" and despite having gained a preliminary sense of the good, it remains vague and out of reach—there in some way, but not for the asking. I may sense possibility, futurity, perhaps even *hope* that there is a way out of my past, my story, but I can't locate it. I may therefore find myself suspended in the difficult and frustrating liminal space of the not-yet, knowing that there is a better way but not knowing quite how to find it. Let us refer to this second stage/state as one of narrative *opening*.

Following this process of narrative opening is a process of *naming*, wherein there emerges a measure of form, positive form, to the goodness one has sensed. A new end is in sight, a new mode of thinking or being that is better than what had been before. In reconstructing my past, therefore, I reconstruct my future as well; I come to realize not only what has gone wrong, but what might be the right way. This can be difficult too, for even though I may have arrived at a clear sense of a better way, I may not have the will or courage or energy to live it. "At fifty-four," Gordon (2003) writes, "there is often nothing to do about regrets but to register them" (p. 32). This is the terrain of the would-have-been: It would have been better to have spent more time with my children, to have said this or done that. But it's past, and, strictly speaking, there is nothing I can do to change it. Hence Gordon, drawing on the existential thinking of Martin Buber, speaks of the " 'irreversibility of lived time' " (p. 32). What's done is done, and I have to live with it.

But there still remains the question of *how* I live with it as well as the challenge of *enacting* the goodness I have named. In short, there remains the question of what I shall make of my past—which, from one perspective, is indeed dead and gone but from another is quite alive. Herein lies the dual meaning of "history": while on the one hand it refers to the facts of the past, marching along, irreversibly, "in" time—the "and then, and then, and then" of clocks and arrows—it also refers to the narrative, the story told about that past. Yes, what's done is done. My father is gone; the episode in Berlin is over, never to return; there is no undoing the fact that Primo Levi and his friend drank that water or that Gordon had written that memoir. It's all *history*. But what shall we make of it? What might the past tell us about the future, and about how we might live?

THE TYRANNY OF MOMENTS

In my view, there no better vehicle for addressing these weighty questions than Tolstoy's harrowing novella, *The Death of Ivan Ilych* (1960 [1886]). Ilych's life "had been most simple and most ordinary and therefore most terrible" (p. 102). Regarded by others as "*le phénix de la famille,*" he had been "an intelligent, polished, lively, and agreeable man" as well as "a capable, cheerful, good-natured, and sociable man, though strict in the fulfillment of what he considered to be his duty: and he considered his duty to be what was considered so by those in authority. Neither as a boy nor as a man was he a toady, but from early youth was by nature attracted to people of high station as a fly is drawn to the light, assimilating their ways and views of life and establishing friendly relations with them." Hindsight had once provided comfort and reassurance to him as well. "At school he had done things which had formerly seemed to him very horrid and made him feel disgusted with himself when he did them; but when later on he saw that such actions were done by people of good position and that they did not regard them as wrong, he was able not exactly to regard them as right, but to forget about them entirely or not be at all troubled at remembering them." Those things weren't so horrid after all; if others think they are okay, then he should too. Following their lead, he would buy clothes at "the fashionable tailor," eat at a "first-class restaurant," and gather whatever else he needed at "the best shops" around (p. 103). Ivan Ilych therefore "performed his official tasks, made his career, and at the same time amused himself pleasantly and decorously." And even in those instances when there had been lapses, "It was all done with clean hands, in clean linen, with French phrases, and above all among people of the best society and consequently with the approval of people of rank" (p. 104). Upon being offered the post of examining magistrate, he continued his successful ways and came to feel that "everyone without exception, even the most important and self-satisfied, was in his power" (p. 105), thereby confirming both his stature and the burgeoning worth of his life.

Ilych's home life told much the same story as his work life. Two years into his new position he met his wife-to-be, "who was the most attractive, clever, and brilliant girl of the set in which he moved, and among other amusements and relaxations from his labours as examining magistrate, Ivan Ilych established light and playful relations with her." At first he had no intention of marrying her; she had simply been a pleasant source of diversion from his demanding work, "but when the girl fell in love with him he said to himself: 'Really, why shouldn't I marry?'" She "came of a good family, was not bad looking, and had some little property," and although he "might have aspired to a more brilliant match, . . . even this was good" (p. 106). All things considered, therefore, getting married had seemed like a most sensible thing to do. "So Ivan Ilych got married" (p. 107).

All went well until his wife's pregnancy, which brought with it "something new, unpleasant, depressing, and unseemly, and from which there was no way of escape" and which led him to realize that "matrimony . . . was not always conducive to the pleasures and amenities of life, but on the contrary often infringed both comfort and propriety" (p. 107). Hence the need "to entrench himself against such infringement [by] . . . securing for himself an existence outside of family life" (p. 108). He was largely successful in this effort, his attitude toward home life rendering him "almost impervious" to the demands it made upon him. "This aloofness might have grieved Ivan Ilych had he considered that it ought not to exist, but he now regarded the position as normal, and even made it the goal at which he aimed in family life." The result was that "The whole interest of his life now centred in the official world and that interest absorbed him, . . . gave him pleasure and filled his life, together with chats with his colleagues, dinners, and bridge. So that on the whole Ivan Ilych's life continued to flow as he considered it should do—pleasantly and properly" (p. 109). There would be some additional rocky periods, to be sure, but in due time his life would regain "its due and natural character of pleasant lightheartedness and decorum" (p. 112), such that "Everything progressed and progressed and approached the ideal he had set himself" (p. 113). What more could one ask of life but that its moments be pleasant ones? What greater ideal could there be?

An accident Ilych suffered while doing some home decorating would disturb all this. It had seemed minor at first, so that "on the whole," still, "his life ran its course as he believed life should do: easily, pleasantly, and decorously" (p. 115). But eventually "this discomfort increased and, though not exactly painful, grew into a sense of pressure in his side accompanied by ill humour. And his irritability became worse and worse and began to mar the agreeable, easy, and correct life" (p. 117) he and his family had established. Not surprisingly, "Ivan Ilych made efforts to force himself to think that he was better" (p. 121). Ultimately, however, "There was no deceiving himself: something terrible, new, and more important than anything before in his life, was taking place within him of which he alone was aware" (p. 122). Indeed, "his life was poisoned and was poisoning the lives of others, and . . . this poison did not weaken but penetrated more and more deeply into his whole being" (p. 124). Having been stripped of the defining features of his life—pleasantness, propriety, correctness—Ilych was suddenly "all alone on the brink of an abyss" (p. 125). "It's not a question of appendix or kidney," he realized, "but of life and . . . death. Yes, life was there and now it is going, going and I cannot stop it" (p. 127). Try as he might "to get back into the former current of thoughts that had once screened the thought of death from him," those lighthearted moments that had felt as if they could go on forever, "all that had formerly shut off, hidden, and destroyed, his consciousness of death, no longer had that effect" (p. 130). The only source of comfort during this dreadful period had been the butler's assistant Gerasim, "a clean, fresh peasant lad, grown stout on town food and always cheerful and bright" (p. 132), who would come to his aid "easily, willingly, simply, and with a good nature that touched Ivan Ilych" (p. 134). But all the while, "the pain remained—that same pain and that same fear that made everything monotonously alike, nothing harder and nothing easier. . . . Again minute followed minute and hour followed hour. Everything remained the same and there was no cessation. And the inevitable end of it all became more and more terrible" (p. 144). One brand of moment had been replaced by quite another.

At one point, in the midst of Ivan Ilych's suffering, there would be a pause. "It was as though he were listening not to an audible voice but to the voice of his soul, to the current of thoughts arising within him" (p. 143). The voice was clear enough: " 'What do you want? What do you want?' " The answer was clear as well: " 'To live and not to suffer,' " and to do so the way he used to, " 'well and pleasantly.' " But as he gazed back at the course of his life it looked different than it had before.

And in imagination he began to recall the best moments of his pleasant life. But strange to say none of those best moments of his pleasant life now seemed at all what they had then seemed— none of them except the first recollections of childhood. There, in childhood, there had been something really pleasant with which it would be possible to live if it could return. But the child who had experienced that happiness existed no longer. It was like a reminiscence of somebody else.

As soon as the period began which produced the present Ivan Ilych, all that had then seemed joys melted before his sight and turned into something trivial and often nasty.

And the further he departed from childhood and the nearer he came to the present the more worthless and doubtful were the joys. (p. 144)

Could it be that those joyful moments were illusory, that his entire life had in fact been quite other than he had imagined it to be?

The Importance of Being Wrong

Faced eventually with the prospect of his own imminent death, Ivan Ilych had found the need to entertain a most disturbing and painful possibility. " 'Maybe I did not live as I ought to have done,' it suddenly occurred to him. 'But how could that be, when I did everything properly?' " He therefore "immediately dismissed from his mind this, the sole solution of all the riddles of life and death, as something quite impossible." Why, then, was he suffering so? "Why, and for what purpose, is there all this horror? But however much he pondered he found no answer. And whenever the thought occurred to him, as it often did, that it all resulted from his not having lived as he ought to have done, he at once recalled the correctness of his whole life and dismissed so strange an idea" (p. 145).

Ivan Ilych is mystified, and continues to find himself searching for a reason: " 'An explanation would be possible if it could be said that I have not lived as I ought to,' " Ilych had tried to convince himself. " 'But it is impossible to say that,' and he remembered all the legality, correctitude, and propriety of his life" (p. 147). Some two weeks later, however, he had found himself facing squarely the possibility in question: " 'What if my whole life has really been wrong?' "

> It occurred to him that what had appeared perfectly impossible before, namely that he had not spent his life as he should have done, might after all be true. It occurred to him that his scarcely perceptible attempts to struggle against what was considered good by the most highly placed people, those scarcely noticeable impulses which he had immediately suppressed, might have been the real thing, and all the rest false. And his professional duties and the whole arrangement of his life and of his family, and all his social and official interests, might all have been false. He tried to defend all those things to himself and suddenly felt the weakness of what he was defending. There was nothing to defend. (p. 149)

What, if anything, could he do in the face of his realization? If there truly was nothing to defend, "and [if] I am leaving this life with the consciousness that I have lost all that was given me and it is impossible to rectify it—what then?' " (p. 149). There is foreclosure, once again, and it appears that he can do nothing at all in the face of it except to avow the truth:

He lay on his back and began to pass his life in review in a new way. In the morning when he saw first his footman, then his wife, then his daughter, and then the doctor, their every word and movement confirmed to him the awful truth that had been revealed to him during the night. In them he saw himself—all that for which he had lived—and saw clearly that it was not real at all, but a terrible and huge deception which had hidden both life and death. This consciousness intensified his physical suffering tenfold. He groaned and tossed about, and pulled at his clothing which choked and stifled him. And he hated them on that account. (p. 149)

Notice here that even though Ivan Ilych has discovered the awful truth about his life, he remains narcissistically encased in the moment. He still cannot see others, only himself ("all that for which he had lived"), and they in turn become the targets of his venomous hatred. After he is convinced to take communion, his wife congratulates him and tries to offer him some comforting words. But, "Her dress, her figure, the expression of her face, the tone of her voice, all revealed the same thing: 'This is wrong, it is not as it should be. All you have lived for and still live for is falsehood and deception, hiding life and death from you.'" With this thought, his hatred surges forth once again, along with his recognition of "the unavoidable, approaching end," and all he can do is shout at her: " 'Go away! Go away and leave me alone!' " (p. 150).

"From that moment the screaming began that continued for three days, and was so terrible that one could not hear it through two closed doors without horror." Ivan Ilych "realized that he was lost, that there was no return, that the end had come, the very end, and his doubts were still unsolved and remained doubts" (p. 150). He is imprisoned in his own foreclosure, and, "For three whole days, during which time did not exist for him, he struggled in that black sack into which he was being thrust by an invisible, resistless force. He struggled as a man condemned to death struggles in the hands of the executioner, knowing that he cannot save himself. And every moment he felt that despite all his efforts he was drawing nearer and nearer to what terrified him." It is here that Ivan Ilych begins to move in the direction of the good: "He felt that his agony was due to his being thrust into that black hole and still more to his not being able to get right into it." Something holds him back, still. "He was hindered from getting into it by his conviction that his life had been a good one. That very justification of his life held him fast and prevented his moving forward, and it caused him most torment of all." But then, suddenly, "some force struck him in the chest and side, making it still harder to breathe, and he fell through the hole and there at the bottom was a light." It was "like the sensation one sometimes experiences in a railway carriage when one thinks one is going backwards while one is really going forwards and suddenly becomes aware of the real direction." Ivan Ilych recognizes the illusion for what is; there thus emerges an opening, an intimation of the good through a recognition of the *not*-good. " 'Yes, it was all not the right thing,' he said to himself, 'but that's no matter. It can be done. But what *is* the right thing?' he asked himself, and suddenly grew quiet.' "

His son stood by the side of his bed, pressed his father's hand to his lips, and began to cry. "At that very moment Ivan Ilych fell through and caught sight of the light, and it was revealed to him that though his life had not been what it should have been, this could still be rectified." But how? Ivan Ilych, seeking to discover the right thing, "grew still, listening. Then he felt that someone was kissing his hand. He opened his eyes, looked at his son, and felt sorry for him. His wife came up to him and he glanced at her. She was gazing at him open-mouthed, with undried tears on her nose and cheek and a despairing look on her face. He felt sorry for her too" (p. 151). The good is being named: from illusion, there is recognition of the "real direction"; from hatred, there is sympathy. It is here that the issue of truth and the issue of goodness come together. Only upon discerning the truth can Ivan Ilych "open his eyes" to others and truly see them, and only upon seeing them— rather than his own hateful projections—can he feel their pain. " 'Yes, I am making them wretched,' he thought" (p. 151). He wants to say something to them. But there must be more than naming and speaking. " 'Besides, why speak? I must act,' he thought." There is not much to be done; he can only try to spare them further wretchedness, and in doing so seek their forgiveness, enough so "that He whose understanding mattered would under-stand" (p. 152). By realizing the truth and by enacting the care that has been called forth by the Other—by the *face* of the Other, as the philosopher Emmanuel Levinas (e.g., 1994, 1999) might put it— Ivan Ilych enters the region of the good.

> And suddenly it grew clear to him that what had been oppres-sing him and would not leave him was all dropping away at once from two sides, from ten sides, and from all sides. He was sorry for them, he must act so as not to hurt them: release them and free himself from these sufferings. "How good and how simple!" he thought. "And the pain?" he asked himself. "What has become of it? Where are you, pain?"
>
> He turned his attention to it.
>
> "Yes, here it is. Well, what of it? Let the pain be."
>
> "And death . . . where is it?"
>
> He sought his former accustomed fear of death and did not find it. "Where is it? What death?" There was no fear because there was no death.

In place of death there was light.

"So that's what it is!" he suddenly exclaimed aloud. "What joy!" (p. 152)

Tolstoy's story is the story of hindsight *par excellence:* having come face to face with the reality of his own imminent death, Ivan Ilych can finally see the "awful truth" of his life. In a distinct sense, he had forgotten to truly see and hear, truly feel, truly *live:* his wife and children had been little more than ornaments or distractions; his job little more than a vehicle for gathering recognition, status, and cheap antiques designed to look expensive; his very self little more than a pitiful replica of the crudest bourgeois success story. So it was that he would approach death not only with regret and shame, as in Primo Levi's case, but also with the most profound horror: to think that all these years he had been living among phantoms, created by his own perversely narcissistic imagination. Only when he could identify his life for what it was could these phantoms assume human form, and only upon assuming human form—by standing forth as the living, breathing, suffering beings they were—could he feel the sort of sympathetic connection that could lead him toward the good.

Narrative Integrity

The fact that Ivan Ilych had to await imminent death before being provoked to survey his life is a telling one. For what it suggests, again, is that he had been living his life unconsciously, unreflectively, his apparent presumption being that death was simply not a concern, that it was essentially irrelevant. To put the matter another way, Ivan Ilych had been living his life without an *ending* in mind; and without any sense of an ending, there could be no story, but only a series of events, experiences, moments, valued for their pleasure or their lack of pain. Other than the condition of its being consonant with social convention and expectation, his life was aimless, devoid of significant purpose and of any organizing principles that might give it meaning. It was thus devoid of what might be called *narrative integrity,*[2] which refers not merely to harmony of proportion or beauty of form but to the soundness and depth of one's ethical and moral commitments, as evidenced by the shape and trajectory of one's life. Ilych, on nearing death, has had revealed to him much more than the fact of his ignorance and superficiality. Also revealed to him is the fact that he has been uncaring and unkind, that he has been so caught up in the niceties of his own small world that reality itself has been obscured, hidden from view. Others have been relegated to the status of *things,* defined essentially by their use value. As significant as his mistreatment of others, however, has been his utter failure to find "devotional objects"—his failure to locate something *outside himself,* outside the perimeter of his immediate experience—that would serve to orient him meaningfully. It is only in the final moments of his life that this occurs, and it is the very condition of his redemption.

But what exactly has happened in this final scene? How are we to make sense of this dramatic movement from "death" to "light"? What seems to have happened is that Ivan Ilych, upon recognizing and avowing the falsity of his previous self-understanding, also recognizes the poverty of his previous moral commitments. This, again, is the destructive moment of narrative reflection. But there

---

[2] See Freeman, 1997b; also Freeman & Brockmeier, 2001.

also exists a creative moment. Indeed, this creative moment is the dialectical counterpart to the destructive: the very fact of Ilych's being able to see, through the dreadful wisdom of hindsight, the patently inferior self he has been means that he has already begun to move beyond it. He had been "wrong," and this implies that there must be a "right." This is not to say, of course, that there is a definitive, absolute way of defining what the right way to live is. Nor is it to say that there is a ready-made formula for living such a life. What is most important, Tolstoy implies, is a willingness to raise the question. " 'What *is* the right thing?' " Ivan Ilych had asked shortly before his death. And in that very moment, Tolstoy told us, he "grew still, listening" (p. 151). Even as Ilych asks the question, he is propelled into an entirely different region of being. It is a region of stillness and silence.

Notice in this context that the act of self-understanding, as it occurs in the dialectical movement at hand, is also an act of self-transcendence; it is an act of divesting oneself of a certain "blind view" of things, of encountering one's own otherness face to face, and, ultimately, of moving on to a more fully realized mode of being human. Notice, in addition, that "rightness" is not something to be *seen* but *heard.* Self-reflection, from this perspective, is never an encounter with the merely neutral "what" of my life; it is an embodied encounter with *me,* a being always seeking to find its proper way. Sometimes this occurs in piecemeal fashion: I move from commitment to commitment but somewhat aimlessly, without a sense of what it's all for. There are also times, however, when something different and much larger may occur. Who am I? we might ask ourselves. Have I been living well? What might it mean to live better? Who should I be? In part, the answers to these questions are tied to the standards, conventions, and moral ideals that inhere in the social worlds we inhabit. But if

Tolstoy is right, there is more to it: the good life, far from being a mere matter of conventional definition or compliance with social norms, can only be articulated through its ultimate value, significance, and worth.

Precarious though our convictions may be, and late though they often are in arriving, "Are we not certain," novelist and philosopher Iris Murdoch (1970) asks, "that there is a 'true direction' toward better conduct, that goodness 'really matters,' and does not that certainty about a standard suggest an idea of permanence which cannot be reduced to psychological or any other set of terms?" (p. 59). "Goodness" is the key term for Murdoch. "The proper and serious use of the term," she maintains, "refers us to a perfection which is perhaps never exemplified in the world we know . . . and which carries with it the ideas of hierarchy and transcendence." In the course of everyday life, "We see differences, we sense directions, and we know that the Good is still somewhere beyond." At one and the same time, it becomes clear that "the self, the place where we live, is a place of illusion. Goodness," therefore, "is connected with the attempt to see the unself, to see and respond to the real world in the light of a virtuous consciousness" (p. 90–91).

What it all comes down to for Murdoch (1970) is that "There is . . . something in the serious attempt to look compassionately at human things which automatically suggests that 'there is more than this.' The 'there is more than this,' if it is not to be corrupted by some sort of quasi-theological finality, must remain a very tiny spark of insight. But . . . the spark is real" (p. 73). It is this spark that suggests that hindsight, when it moves in the direction of self-reckoning, sometimes relies on standards and ideals that "cannot be reduced to psychological or any other set of empirical terms." There is something transcendent, something *more*. William James also has some interesting and provocative things to say about this idea of the "more" in *The Varieties of Religious Experience* (1985 [1902]) when he notes that, "The individual, so far as he suffers from his wrongness and criticises it, is to that extent consciously beyond it, and in at least possible touch with something higher, . . . a better part of him, even though it may be but a most helpless germ" (p. 508). Not unlike Murdoch and James, I posit this not out of faith per se but out of my reading of stories like Primo Levi's, Tolstoy's, and others which suggest that, in the process of looking backward over the course of one's life, the evaluative stakes are frequently very high—higher, in fact, than a purely "immanent" account might lead one to believe. One might again speak in this context of the *transcendent horizon* of the life story. This is surely one of Tolstoy's main messages in *The Death of Ivan Ilych*. The good life cannot be a mere matter of convention, of compliance with social norms, but rather emerges against the backdrop of ultimate concerns. This is the good news: if Tolstoy is right, *we know what goodness is.*[3] Indeed, we know—even if incompletely and imperfectly— what is of true value, significance, and worth; it is this "tiny spark of insight," as Murdoch put it, that orients and conditions the very movement of our lives.

But Tolstoy's story carries another, decidedly more tragic message as well, and it has to do with the fact that it is perilously easy for human beings, fallible as we are, to *forget* what is of true value, significance, and worth and to substitute what is transient, momentary, merely a matter of social convention and propriety. According to Heidegger (1962 [1927]), among others, this forgetfulness about life is intimately tied to our anxiety about

[3] See Freeman, 1997b.

death, along with our anxious refusal to admit its inevitability for us. Consider the sentiments of Ivan Ilych's colleagues as they learn of his death: "Besides considerations as to the possible transfers and promotions likely to result from Ivan Ilych's death, the mere fact of the death of a near acquaintance aroused, as usual, in all who heard of it the complacent feeling that, 'it is he who is dead and not I' " (p. 94–95). Death was something that "had happened to Ivan Ilych," one of his ("so-called") friends had thought, "and not to him, and that it should not and could not happen to him, and that to think that it could would be yielding to depression." It was "as though death was an accident natural to Ivan Ilych but certainly not to himself" (p. 102).

Heidegger (1962 [1927]) writes:

> In the publicness with which we are with one another in our everyday manner, death is "known" as a mishap which is constantly occurring—as "a case of death." Someone or other "dies," be he neighbor or stranger. People who are no acquaintances of ours are "dying" daily and hourly. "Death" is encountered as a well-known event occurring within-the-world. As such it remains in the inconspicuousness characteristic of what is encountered in an everyday fashion. The "they" have already stowed away an interpretation for this event. It talks of it in a "fugitive" manner, either expressly or else in a way which is mostly inhibited, as if to say, "One of these days one will die too, in the end; but right now it has nothing to do with us." (pp. 296–297)

Heidegger thus comes to speak of "evasive concealment in the face of death" (p. 297) and of the notion that the "they," *das Man,* the anonymous mass of others, caught up in the flow of moments, operating under the tacit assumption that these moments can go on forever, "covers up what is peculiar in death's certainty—*that it is possible at any moment*" (p. 302).

I might also turn to another font of wisdom, my (then) nine-year-old daughter. "How old do you think you'll be when you die?" she asked me one night as I was putting her to bed. "I don't know, honey," I responded. "I wonder if I'll die before you," she mused. "Oh, God," I moaned. "I hope not." "I hope not too," she then said, "*but you never ever know.*" She was not at all morose or anxious talking about death; she was simply uttering what for her was a truism, and on she went to the next series of nighttime thoughts, about what she would wear to school the next day, her lunch, and so on. I, meanwhile, held her tight, in desperation almost, the inevitability of our deaths and the uncertainty of their timing suddenly emerging with that kind of force we only rarely allow ourselves to encounter. And in that very instant I was moved to think about my life, especially as it related to my daughter, who at any moment might be gone, and to ask whether indeed it was what it ought to be.

Other events force us to raise much the same question: accidents, killing sprees where the innocent are victims, even happy events such as vacations, which sometimes separate us from those we love. More than these events, however, it is death itself, in its multiple manifestations, that insists that the question be asked. We therefore find a deep link between death and what I earlier called narrative integrity, the well-lived life embodying a story worthy of being told. A qualification may be in order here. In speaking of a story worthy of being told, I do not wish to suggest that our lives must be exciting or mysterious or heroic or that they should be worthy of being packaged and sold in corner stores for their great appeal. Nor do I wish to suggest that our lives must embody wholly coherent, artfully patterned, wrinkle-free narratives; enough has been written about the disintegration of the modern and postmodern self to render this picture suspect if not utterly incongruous with our present situation. Rather, I am underscoring the importance of being "present" enough to our own lives, mindful enough of our own inclination to forgetfulness, that we make good use of the limited time we have. Narrative integrity therefore requires considerable vigilance. But of what sort?

In the preceding pages, I have suggested that the value of hindsight is partly a function of the human tendency toward lateness, particularly in the moral realm. A kind of temporal slippage exists, a "lag," between experience and memory. This lag, I have also suggested, can never be eliminated entirely; it is part and parcel of human being-in-time. There is thus a dimension of hindsight, along with the narrative figuration and refiguration of the past, that is patently unsurpassable. When I am living largely in the moment, Ivan Ilych-style, I cannot easily discern the overall pattern of my life; insofar as I become caught up in the immediacy of things, it recedes into the background of experience. This is not to say that immediate moments cannot be meaningful; if we are fortunate, we will have many wonderful, memorable moments throughout our lives. But the idea here is that distance from these moments, and from longer periods of our lives—and from "our lives" themselves, taken as a whole—allows us the opportunity to see things that we were unable to see, or unable to see clearly, at the time of their occurrence. Another way of saying this is that "visibility," factually speaking, of the sort that exists in moments, is often correlative with *in*visibility, metaphorically speaking: my immersion in the moment, perhaps in virtue of its radiance and brightness, can blind me to "the big picture." The process of my life becoming visible, in turn, is contingent upon my stepping out of that moment and turning my gaze to the landscape of the past. Judging from the story of Ivan Ilych, this process can be perilous indeed. It can also be reinvigorating and redemptive, serving to correct the shortsightedness of the present and thereby open up new vistas of being.

What becomes available through temporal distance, it must be emphasized, is not only the more panoramic view of things just considered but a *narrative context*—that is, a context within which one can situate the various episodes of one's life in relation to one another and to the emerging whole. It is with these two dimensions of temporal distance in mind that Gadamer (1975) speaks of it as potentially positive and productive (see also Chapter 6). I say "potentially" for one basic reason; and that is, even though I *may* achieve an enhanced understanding of certain features of experience by virtue of my distance from them, I may also achieve a quite distorted understanding, in line, perhaps, with what I refuse to see or am unable to see, still. Temporal distance is therefore no automatic remedy for confusion or delusion; nor is it a sure ticket to the truth. But it is only in hindsight, through narrative reflection, that one is in a position to survey the whole that is one's life; it is only through such survey that there exists the possibility of discerning the truth about that life, indefinite and ungraspable though it is; and it is only through discerning the truth that one is able to move, surely and securely, in the direction of the good. We can only hope to engage in this process a bit earlier in our own lives than Ivan Ilych did in his. But how? How, short of staring death in the face, can we possibly rise to the challenge at hand?

DEATH, DISTANCE, AND DEVELOPMENT

Somehow, we need to achieve that sort of self-distancing, often achieved only in the face of death, that can orient us vigilantly to what is of true value in our lives. This ought not to be construed merely as a plea for "personal authenticity," if by that we are referring to the aim "being true to myself," alone. Important though this sometimes is, it is not fundamentally what the story of Ivan Ilych is about. Nor, I would venture, is it what most of our own stories are about. As Taylor notes in *The Ethics of Authenticity* (1991), there is indeed a tendency within modernity to emphasize, and valorize, this aim. "Being true to myself," he writes, "means being true to my own originality, and that is something only I can articulate and discover. In articulating it, I am also defining myself. I am realizing a potential that is properly my own" (p. 29). What Taylor wants to show, however, is that thinking about authenticity without regard to the demands of our ties to others or to demands "emanating from something more or other than human desires or aspirations" (p. 35) is self-defeating and, on some level, meaningless. Things take on importance against a background, a horizon, of intelligibility. "Even the sense that the significance of my life comes from its being chosen . . . depends on the understanding that *independent of my will* there is something noble, courageous, and hence significant in giving shape to my own life." Authenticity, therefore, "is not the enemy of demands that emanate from beyond the self; it supposes such demands" (p. 41).

Along these lines, the task of orienting oneself to what is of true value may be thought of in terms of one's relatedness to what I earlier called "devotional objects" *outside the self.*[4] These may be gods or responsibilities or significant projects, and, if Levinas is right, they will almost certainly involve other people, whose existence—whose very *face*—often immediately informs

[4] See especially Levinas, 1994.

us about what is of true value. [5] Consider Ivan Ilych, who in the midst of asking what the "right thing" in life might be and "listening" for a response, felt his son kiss his hand. Upon opening his eyes, it was as if he was *seeing* the people in his life for the first time. Paradoxically, he had to listen carefully for this to occur: their faces, we might say, *spoke* to him. The face of death had revealed to him, however briefly, the face of the Other in its sacred, pitiful presence.

But again, how, short of staring death in the face, might we achieve the needed self-distancing? One "method," such as it is, would be to undertake a thought experiment of the sort Nietzsche (1974 [1887]) presents through his notion of the eternal return:

> What if some day or night a demon were to steal after you into your loneliest loneliness and say to you: "This life as you now live it and have lived it, you will have to live once more and innumerable times more; and there will be nothing new in it, but every pain and every joy and every thought and sigh and everything unutterably small or great in your life will have to return to you, all in the same succession and sequence—even this spider and this moonlight between the trees, and even this moment and I myself. The eternal hourglass of existence is turned upside down again and again, and you with it, speck of dust!" Would you not throw yourself down and gnash your teeth and curse the demon who spoke thus? Or have you once experienced a tremendous moment when you would have

[5] As noted earlier, Levinas is the foremost philosopher of the "face," which, for him, is the very source of our responsiveness and responsibility to others. For an introduction to his ideas, see Levinas, 1985; for a more recent version, see Levinas, 1999.

answered him: "You are a god and never have I heard anything more divine." (pp. 273–274)

Nietzsche's thought experiment is a valuable one for present purposes; it provokes us into taking stock of our lives and perhaps even changing them, doing what is needed to ensure that our own response to this hypothetical demon would be an affirmative one. Yet there are at least two significant problems in his formulation. First, even though Nietzsche is speaking in this passage of "every pain and every joy and every thought and sigh," he is not really speaking about one's life *as a whole*. That is, he is not considering it as a whole phenomenon, possessed of narrative integrity, but instead as a sequence of experiences which, like a string of beads, is either colorful enough to be worn again and again or so dull and lusterless as to be disposable. The second problem, which very much follows from the first, is that even if we grant that Nietzsche is on some level interested in considering the phenomenon of a whole life, he is manifestly less interested in considering the phenomenon of a *good* life. This is hardly a shocking revelation about Nietzsche's work. Not only is it generally more about pleasure and pain than virtue; much of it seeks to take us "beyond good and evil" (Nietzsche, 1966 [1886]) altogether. What is finally at work is "the will to power," Nietzsche (1968 [1888]) tells us; and how well we are able to exercise this will—whether we shrink in the face of the challenge before us or grow larger and stronger— determines how "good" our life ultimately is.

Narrative integrity is thus largely irrelevant, if not unthinkable, from Nietzsche's perspective. In fact, he would more than likely see it as a rather quaint idea, tied, perhaps, to some of those very idols he was most interested in destroying. If Tolstoy is right, however, narrative integrity is a much sounder organizing principle for our lives than the will to power. Ivan Ilych "had it all"; he had in fact taken great pleasure in his being able to orchestrate the life of his dreams, to craft himself and his world in a way that seemed to correspond to his fancied images of what it was supposed to be like. But in the end, he wound up suffering a great deal. In any case, valuable though Nietzsche's thought experiment may be, some significant difficulties are involved in the process as well.

Are there other possibilities? I have spoken of hindsight as a much-needed "corrective" to the limits of the present. Perhaps there is a way of somehow framing this corrective dimension in preventative form. The method here would in effect be to *anticipate our recollections*—that is, to project ourselves into the future, looking backward, and to imagine the kind of story we would hope to be able to tell as death draws near. This formulation is not without its difficulties either. Recall Emily Fox Gordon's lament about having written her memoir "from an impossibly posthumous point of view, as if I knew the final truth of my life" (2004, p. 26). Stuart Charmé (1984) also suggests that a certain audacity is involved in trying to discern the meaning and significance of one's life before it has ended: "a person can never achieve that fixed view of the end which could solidify the meaning of the present" (p. 252); it is like leaping over the course of time. Indeed, the full meaning of the present, Charmé implies, can only issue after death, after there has emerged the ending to which all previous episodes have led. But in this case, of course, only others will be able to survey the whole; it will be rather too late for oneself. The long and short of the difficulties at hand is that they are real: strictly speaking, there is no way to know one's own story until it is over. But let us not be overly strict; if Ivan Ilych's terrible demise is any indication, there surely remains value in trying, as best one can, to live the kind of life one would look back upon without shuddering in shame or despair.

Earlier on in this chapter, drawing on Taylor's *Sources of the Self* (1989), we noted a connection between some "orientation to the good," which he considered an "ineradicable" feature of human life, and the process of narrative reflection. Indeed, "This sense of the good," he told us, "has to be woven into my life as an unfolding story," and this unfolding story points in the direction of my story-to-come as a function of its perceived value and worth. As such, I will either "endorse" the given direction or chart a new one, one that is more in keeping with my emerging sense of the good. In speaking of this unfolding story, revisioned and revised in accordance with an orientation to the good, Taylor is speaking about what is colloquially known in psychological circles as the process of *development*.[6] How might we understand this process?

Taylor describes development—although not by that name—as a process of "reasoning in transitions," one that "aims to establish, not that some position is correct but rather that some position is superior to some other." This mode of reasoning is thus "concerned, covertly or openly, implicitly or explicitly, with comparative propositions." But there is more to it as well. "This form of argument," he adds, "has its source in biographical narrative. We are convinced that a certain view is superior because we have lived a transition which we understand as error-reducing and hence as epistemic gain. I see that I was confused about the relation of resentment and love, or I see that

---

[6] For many years, I have attempted (with varying degrees of success!) to think through the relationship between the idea of narrative and the idea of development. For examples, see Freeman, 1984, 1985, 1991, 1993; also Freeman and Robinson, 1990.

there is a depth to love conferred by time, which I was quite insensitive to before" (p. 72). The process of development, therefore, relies on hindsight, on being able to "see" the error of our earlier ways and, in this seeing, to "gain" from it. Its connotations of "progress" notwithstanding, development is therefore as much about the *past* as it is about the future.

Equally paradoxical is the fact that it is as much about the *Other* as it is about the self. In addition to "supersession"—the replacement of an inferior view or mode of being with a better one, there also emerge what Taylor calls "hypergoods"—which consist of those "higher-order goods [that] not only are incomparably more important than others but provide the standpoint from which these must be weighed, judged, decided about" (p. 63). In sum: "If hypergoods arise through supersessions, the conviction they carry comes from our reading of the transitions to them, from a certain understanding of moral growth" (p. 72). This reading remains open to challenge; there will be further supersessions, further realizations both of one's own failings and the hypergoods they imply. There will be cycles of tragic humility and redemptive reparation, profound loss and momentous gain. All of this is bound up with the narrative order, which, in turn, emerges out of the temporality of hindsight.

I would reframe Taylor's idea by suggesting that, rather than hypergoods arising through supersessions, it is just the opposite: supersessions arise through hypergoods, through some sphere of goodness—some *Other,* outside the perimeter of the self—that draws the developmental process forward. Upon asking what the right way was, Ivan Ilych had finally encountered the Other face to face, and upon this encounter he would be able, finally, to catch sight of the light and move toward it. As we have seen through his story, the distance between his earlier life and his emerging understanding seemed initially to be utterly unbridgeable. There had been development, to be sure; the very fact of his being able to see the awful truth of his past was a step along the way. But it was only the beginning of the developmental process, and the new-found awareness he had acquired had "intensified his physical suffering tenfold," resulting in a profoundly painful sense of narrative foreclosure. Subsequently, there would need to be a process of narrative *opening*, which would provide a glimpse of a better way; one of *naming*, wherein he would identify and articulate this better way; and, finally, one of *enacting* it in the few moments that remained in his life. We should not forget, of course, that Tolstoy's story is a work of fiction, that Ivan Ilych is but a character in the story, and that horrific despair doesn't always end in redemption and repair. There is nevertheless much to be learned from Tolstoy's extraordinary tale.

IN THE DIRECTION OF THE GOOD

On one level, the "developmental narrative" we have been considering is to be attributed to the self. In a most basic and obvious sense, narratives issue from an individual person: the story of my life is thus irrevocably *mine*. This says nothing whatsoever, though, about the ultimate sources of my story, about the driving forces that propel it forward, giving it meaning and substance. These forces cannot, and do not, derive from the self but instead derive from the Other. Along these lines, it might plausibly be said that while the *proximal* source of personal narrative is the self, the *distal* source is the Other. Indeed, it might also be said—cautiously—that the Other is the distal source of selfhood itself.[7] In Ivan Ilych's

---

[7] For example, Freeman, 2007. For explorations of the "Other," see Levinas, 1985, 1996; also Gantt & Williams, 2002; Sampson, 1993.

case, it is the presence of flesh and blood others who bring him back to himself, as a feeling, responsive, and responsible being; they are the inspiration for his development, his coming-into-goodness.

As suggested earlier, the human Other is not the only source of such inspiration. According to Iris Murdoch especially (e.g., 1970, 1993), numerous other "objects of attention"—art, nature, God, even the idea of goodness itself—serve to draw the self outward, beyond its own borders.[8] What is key is the idea of *relatedness* to some Other, whether human or nonhuman, that can serve as a point of orientation and direction for the process of discerning the direction of one's life. Drawing on Plato, "Life," Murdoch (1993) writes, "is a spiritual pilgrimage inspired by the disturbing magnetism of *truth*, involving *ipso facto* a purification of energy and desire in the light of a vision of what is *good*. The good and just life is thus a process of clarification, a movement toward selfless lucidity, guided by ideas of perfection which are objects of *love*" (p. 14). As Murdoch goes on to note, "There are innumerable points at which we have to detach ourselves, to change our orientation, to redirect our desire and refresh and purify our energy, to keep on looking in the right direction" (p. 25). Hindsight is a key player in the process; it is precisely the pause that refreshes. And, anything but the cold-blooded act of pure cognition it is sometimes imagined to be, it is fueled by *eros,* "the continuous operation of spiritual energy, desire, intellect, love, as it moves among and responds to particular objects of attention" (p. 496).

It is quite possible that some readers are growing uncomfortable with this line of thinking. What exactly is Murdoch saying

---

[8] See also Simone Weil's (1997 [1952]) *Gravity and Grace.*

here? Why "love"? Murdoch's answer is reminiscent of Tolstoy's. The fact is, "People speak of loving all sorts of things, their work, a book, a potted plant, a formation of clouds. Desire for what is corrupt and worthless, the degradation of love, its metamorphosis into ambition, vanity, cruelty, greed, jealousy, hatred, or the parched demoralising deserts of its absence, are phenomena often experienced and readily recognised." At a very basic level, therefore, "People know the difference between good and evil, it takes quite a lot of theorising to persuade them to say or imagine that they do not" (pp. 496–497). How else could Ivan Ilych have known that his life had been so terribly wrong? This does not mean that we can articulate easily what goodness is or that we can speak cogently about it or that it is singular in its nature; Tolstoy himself only gives us the barest clues, most often via the route of failures and pathologies, about what it might conceivably be. Indeed, as the story of Ivan Ilych shows, it seems much easier to identify what goodness is *not* than to identify what it is. But there is no mistaking its presence. It is, once more, a region we can enter and inhabit, by degrees.

It is here, in this notion of "degrees," that we can begin to link up some of Murdoch's thoughts regarding the good with the process of development and the work of hindsight. "Is it important to measure and compare things and know just how good they are?" Yes, Murdoch answers. "A deep understanding of any field of human activity (painting, for instance) involves an increasing revelation of degrees of excellence and often a revelation of there being in fact little that is very good and nothing that is perfect." Moreover, "Increasing understanding of human conduct operates in a similar way. We come to perceive scales, distances, standards, and may incline to see as less than excellent what previously we were prepared to 'let by'" (1970, p. 61). Notice in this final sentence that a dimension of *correction* is involved, in which one rethinks and reevaluates one's earlier view of things through having arrived at a better place. And what this implies, again, is that development—movement in the direction of the good, inspired by what is Other—is intimately and necessarily linked to hindsight, that is, to the capacity to look back on an earlier mode of knowing or being and to realize its poverty.

Just as the recognition of illusion bespeaks an intimation of the truth, so too does the recognition of moral poverty bespeak an intimation of the good. Even though Ilych does finally "see the light," we may assume that it was still quite dim, lit perhaps only by the tiny spark about which Murdoch had spoken. He had merely "caught sight of it," but this was quite enough to move him forward. In speaking of "the good" and "the good life," therefore, I wish to offer one final reminder that I am speaking of just this sort of dimly lit region, to be entered and reentered but without ever arriving at a final destination. From one angle, this might seem despairing: save death, there is no discrete and definitive end in sight; it is forever out of reach, postponed, deferred. From another angle, though, it is the very *open-endedness* of the process of living, and the possibility of correcting, and correcting again, our view of things that serves to deepen moral life. That the process is an infinite one is surely a good thing; for, without a final point of arrival, we can be sure that there will still remain ample room to move and that hindsight will remain a key player in the process.

Coda: Hindsight and Beyond

I n view of what we have learned throughout the preceding pages, it might be said that one of the foremost challenges we face as human beings is to diminish the "lag" between past and present, experience and hindsight. This can be achieved through thought experiments of the sort considered earlier, which involve anticipating one's recollections and living accordingly. Along these lines, it is important at times to pause and to ask: What will this experience—this anger, this immovable conviction, this impulsive assertion—look like when I revisit it at some future point in time? And, following Tolstoy, how will it look on the eve of my death? Tolstoy is hardly alone in raising this question. "For you know, Socrates," Cephalus says in the opening pages of *The Republic* (2003),

> when a man faces death there come into his mind anxieties that did not trouble him before. The stories about another world, and about punishment in a future life for wrongs done in this, at which he once used to laugh, begin to torment his mind with the fear that they might be true. And either because of the weakness of old age or because, as he approaches the other world, he has some clearer perception of it, he is filled with

doubts and fears and begins to reckon up and see if there is anyone he has wronged. The man who finds that in the course of his life he has done a lot of wrong often wakes up at night in terror, like a child with a nightmare, and his life is full of foreboding: but the man who is conscious of no wrongdoing is filled with cheerfulness and with hope, "the comfort of old age," as Pindar calls it. (pp. 6–7)

Judging from this passage, along with the story of Ivan Ilych, it is death and death alone that brings about a "clearer perception" of our former ways and incites our need to "reckon up." By doing what we can to project ourselves into this future moment, perhaps we can avoid the night terrors of which Cephalus speaks.

Is there any other way? Is it possible to somehow bypass or circumvent the work of hindsight? Strictly speaking, the answer is "no," for as noted earlier, some aspects of hindsight are patently unsurpassable. Even if I were to acquire the capacity to look at the reality of my life straightaway, such that I could see everything that was going on at any given moment, I still would not know how the meaning of that moment would unfold. For that, I would have to await future moments, future episodes, to see what has gone on; only then would I know—and only provisionally—its meaning and significance, its "role" in the evolving story of my life. There is no getting beyond this dimension of hindsight and narrative reflection; it is part and parcel of the temporality of being human.

And yet: there is no question but that the aforementioned lag between experience and hindsight can sometimes be diminished. The challenge is to live mindfully enough of the present, and of the limits of one's perspective, to allow more adequate or comprehensive perspectives into view. How can this be done?

Throughout the story of Ivan Ilych, we encounter superficial-
ities, illusions, and outright lies, and it becomes clear that Ilych's
own insatiable ego has been the main culprit, poisoning and
even obliterating reality. There is no relationship to what is
Other, whether person or world, and no sustenance, no nour-
ishment; there is only Self, foisting its own needs and wishes
onto whomever and whatever comes its way. It is only at the
very end of the story, when he admits the error of his ways, that
reality comes into focus. And it is only when reality comes into
focus that there emerges sympathy for the others around him. If
only he could have seen them earlier! But this is exactly what he
could not do. "By opening our eyes," Murdoch (1970) has
written, "we do not necessarily see what confronts us." On her
account, "We are anxiety-ridden animals. Our minds are con-
tinually active, fabricating an anxious, usually self-preoccupied,
often falsifying veil which partially conceals the world" (p. 82).
But there remains hope, manifested in those occasional intimations of reality—and goodness—that creep through the veil.

A fundamental premise of this book has been that one of the
most valuable vehicles for correcting this falsifying concealment
is hindsight itself. But again, what about other methods, of a
more preventative sort, that might serve to diminish the intensity of the moral rescue mission hindsight so often performs?
"Are there any techniques for the purification and reorientation
of an energy which is naturally selfish, in such a way that when
moments of choice arrive we shall be sure of acting rightly?"
(Murdoch, 1970, p. 53). Murdoch's question is fraught with
difficulties. The notion of "techniques" is problematic in its
own right, and were they to exist it would be strange, and tragic,
that we have yet to discover them. Also questionable is
Murdoch's supposition regarding our "naturally selfish"
energy. There is little doubt about the human potential for

selfishness, but whether it is a natural attribute is less clear. Finally, can we *ever* be sure of acting rightly? These difficulties notwithstanding, Murdoch's basic question remains. How, if at all, can we make ourselves morally better?

Traditionally, one way of doing so is through the various techniques of religion, particularly prayer. Whatever else may be going on as one prays, and whatever else God may be, she/he/it exists as an "object of attention," a "source of energy" that, for some at any rate, serves indeed to purify and reorient their own ego-centered preoccupations. "That God, attended to, is a powerful source of (often good) energy is a psychological fact" (p. 54). For Murdoch, however, the most valuable objects of attention are found in art and nature. Indeed, "The appreciation of beauty in art or nature is not only (for all its difficulties) the easiest available spiritual exercise; it is also a completely adequate entry into the good life, since it *is* the checking of selfishness in the interest of seeing the real." As she goes on to note, "Of course great artists are 'personalities' and have special styles," particularly (as we saw in Chapter 5) in the modern era. "But the greatest art," she insists, "is 'impersonal' because it shows us the world, our world and not another one, with a clarity which startles and delights us simply because we are not used to looking at the real world at all" (p. 63). Moreover, "it teaches us how real things can be looked at and loved without being seized and used, without being appropriated into the greedy organism of the self" (p. 64). Ivan Ilych might certainly have benefited from this sort of art! Indeed, it may well have obviated some of the reconstructive labor that had emerged as he approached his own demise.

But a potential element of virtue also is involved in the very act of attending, whatever the object: "This exercise of *detachment*," Murdoch continues, "is difficult and valuable whether the thing contemplated is a human being or the root of a tree or the vibration of a colour or a sound. Unsentimental contemplation of nature exhibits the same quality of detachment: selfish concerns vanish, nothing exists except the things which are seen" (p. 64). Murdoch calls this process "unselfing," and sees it as a key to moral life.

> I am looking out of my window in an anxious and resentful state of mind, oblivious of my surroundings, brooding perhaps on some damage done to my prestige. Then suddenly I observe a hovering kestrel. In a moment everything is altered. The brooding self with its hurt vanity has disappeared. There is nothing now but kestrel. And when I return to thinking of the other matter it seems less important. And of course this is something which we may also do deliberately: give attention to nature in order to clear our minds of selfish care. (p. 82)

I am not sure whether "detachment" is the best word to use in describing this sort of contemplative relationship to nature; "relatedness" or "responsiveness" or "open attentiveness" might do better. But the idea remains: the very act of attending, fully, to what is other-than-self, serves to check and diminish our own selfish impulses. It may provide a spur to moral action as well. This is particularly so when the objects of our attention are other people. For "the more the separateness and differentness of other people is realized, and the fact seen that another person has needs and wishes as demanding as one's own, the harder it becomes to treat a person as a thing" (p. 64). Perhaps Ivan Ilych could have done without great works of art after all. More than anything, he needed to see who and what had been *there*, before him. I emphasize "before": had he been able to truly see them, he would have realized that they had priority, and by doing

so—that is, by recognizing their separateness and differentness—he would have better realized not only their humanity
but his own.

Attention, like hindsight, is therefore a corrective device, a
vehicle not so much of detachment but of distance, *productive*
distance, that can allow us to see that which we were unable to
see before. It too is thus a vehicle of disclosure, revelation,
unconcealment, and can serve much the same sorts of developmental functions that hindsight serves. Indeed, the virtues of
attention that Murdoch and others have identified are themselves applicable to the work of hindsight. From the very start,
we have noted that hindsight can be, and frequently is, a source
of distortion and falsification. Moreover, just as the myriad
needs of the self can obscure the reality of the moment, so too
can it obscure the reality of the past, blinding us to what it has to
say. Recall what was said toward the end of Chapter 6 regarding
the importance of *listening,* attentively and open-mindedly, to
the personal past. It is so easy to foist meaning onto it, to corrupt
it with our designs and desires—so much so, in fact, that this
very foisting, this imposition of meaning has come to be seen by
many as the natural order of things. There is some truth to this
idea, if only for the fact that I cannot possibly discern the reality
of my past without bringing certain "prejudices" to it: I can only
see and hear what I am prepared to see and hear, by my
language, my culture, by the *world* I am already inhabiting.
This preparedness is in fact the very condition of my seeing and
hearing; it is what orients me to this feature of the past rather
than that, and what allows me to "make sense" of things. But
none of this entails the necessity of imposing meaning onto the
past and thereby distorting and falsifying it. The degree to
which I do so is, in part, a function of the state of my ego and
of what I need to see in the story of my life. Like Ivan Ilych,

I may need to see it as being just "as it should be," pleasant and carefree, if only to defend against my own superficiality. But how I relate to my past is also a function of the quality of attention I bring to it, whether it allows me to "pierce the veil" of my own needful imaginings.

In the Introduction to this book, I noted that meditative and mindfulness practices entail a marked focus on the *now*. There may also be talk of the disturbing, even destructive, nature of the stories we bring to bear on our own understandings; we can get caught up in them, trapped, persistently seeing the world through the filter of our too-redundant mythic tales about who and what we are. There is unquestionably some truth to this. But the problem isn't stories per se. It is with those that entrap us and prevent us from seeing what is really there. Hindsight thus requires mindfulness in its own right. In a sense, in fact, it requires a kind of respectful attention to the "separateness and differentness" of one's own self, even a capacity to behold "oneself as another," as Paul Ricoeur (1992) has put it. It is not easy to achieve, and may need to be *cultivated,* in much the same way that meditative and mindfulness practices are. But it will be well worth the effort. For, as I have tried to show throughout the pages of this book, hindsight is a vitally important vehicle not only for "knowing thyself," but through this knowing, for fashioning and refashioning the very ends of life.

BIBLIOGRAPHIC NOTE

In this bibliographic note, I deal exclusively with books, including edited volumes, and concentrate my attention mainly on those works that address matters of memory, narrative, identity, and related issues in the context of the study of lives. The literature on narrative is now vast, and ranges from "big-story" approaches such as my own (i.e., more "macro" approaches that look toward significant episodes, portions of a life, or even the whole of a life, through such vehicles as biographical, autobiographical, and fictional writing, interviews, and clinical encounters) all the way to "small-story" approaches (i.e., those that are more "micro" in orientation and that generally derive from the careful recording and analysis of everyday social exchanges). For a good and comprehensive review of the range of approaches found in narrative inquiry, see especially Bamberg's edited collection, *Narrative: State of the Art* (2007).

Other recent (2000 and after) volumes include Andrews et al.'s (edited) *Lines of Narrative: Psychosocial Perspectives* (2000), *The Uses of Narrative: Explorations in Sociology, Psychology, and Cultural Studies* (2004), and *Doing Narrative Research* (2008); Bamberg and Andrews' (edited) *Considering Counter-Narratives: Narrating, Resisting, Making Sense* (2004); Brockmeier and Carbaugh's (edited) *Narrative and Identity: Studies in Autobiography, Self and Culture* (2001); Bruner's *Making Stories: Law, Literature, Life* (2003); Butler's *Giving an Account of Oneself* (2005); Clandinin's (edited) *Handbook of Narrative Inquiry: Mapping a Methodology* (2006); Daiute and Lightfoot's (edited) *Narrative Analysis: Studying the Development of Individuals in Society* (2003); Eakin's *Living Autographically: How We Create Identity in Narrative* (2008); Fireman et al.'s (edited) *Narrative and Consciousness: Literature, Psychology, and the Brain* (2003); Fivush and Haden's (edited) *Autobiographical Memory and the Construction of a Narrative Self: Developmental and Cultural Perspectives* (2003); Hoerl and McCormack's (edited) *Time and Memory: Issues in Philosophy and Psychology* (2001); Holstein and Gubrium's *The Self We Live By: Narrative Identity in a Postmodern World* (2000); Josselson et al.'s (edited) *The Meaning of Others: Narrative Studies of Relationships* (2007); Kearney's *On Stories* (2001); King's *Memory, Narrative, Identity: Remembering the Self* (2000); Lieblich et al.'s (edited) *Healing Plots: The Narrative Basis of Psychotherapy* (2004); McAdams' *The Redemptive Self: Stories Americans Live By* (2005) and McAdams et al.'s (edited) *Identity and Story: Creating Self in Narrative* (2006) and *Turns in the Road: Narrative Studies of Lives in Transition* (2001); Muldoon's *Tricks of Time: Bergson, Merleau-Ponty and Ricoeur in Search of Time, Self and Meaning* (2006); Olney's *Memory and Narrative: The Weave of Life-Writing* (2000); Patterson's (edited) *Strategic Narrative: New Perspectives on the Power of Personal and Cultural Stories* (2002); Ricoeur's *Memory, History, Forgetting* (2006); and Riessman's *Narrative Methods for the Human Sciences* (2007).

There are other volumes I might have included as well. Some of them I don't know well enough to list, some of them I don't know at all, and, not least, some of them I have no doubt forgotten or omitted by mistake. To those of you whose works fall into these categories, please accept my apologies. It should also be noted that many other books bear on the present issues that were written or edited before 2000, but in the interest of brevity, I have not included them, deciding, quite arbitrarily, to stay with those published in 2000 or after.

Finally, of course, there is an enormous volume of relevant articles in journals such as *Narrative Inquiry, Theory & Psychology, Culture and Psychology,* and numerous other qualitatively oriented venues. Rather than attempting to enumerate them here, I simply encourage interested readers to scan the contents of these journals and see what's there. Whether or not work in this burgeoning area of inquiry constitutes a bona fide intellectual "movement" is for others to decide. But in terms of both quantity and quality, the material that has emerged is extraordinary and signals the advance of a more fully human way of exploring the human condition.

REFERENCES

Allan, G. (1993). Traditions and transitions. In P. Cook (Ed.), *Philosophical Imagination and Cultural Memory* (pp. 21–39). Durham, NC: Duke University Press.

Andrews, M. (2007). *Shaping History: Narratives of Political Change*. Cambridge, UK: Cambridge University Press.

Andrews, M., Sclater, S.D., Squire, C., & Treacher, A. (Eds.). (2000). *Lines of Narrative: Psychosocial Perspectives*. London: Routledge.

Andrews, M., Sclater, S.D., Squire, C., & Treacher, A. (Eds.). (2004). *The Uses of Narrative: Explorations in Sociological, Psychological, and Cultural Studies*. London: Routledge.

Andrews, M., Squire, C., & Tamboukou, M. (Eds.). (2008). *Doing Narrative Research*. Beverly Hills, CA: Sage.

Aristotle. (1973). *Poetics*. Ann Arbor, MI: University of Michigan Press. (Originally sometime between the 360s and the 320s, B.C.)

Augustine. (1980). *Confessions*. New York: Penguin. (Originally 397)

Bamberg, M. (2006). Stories: Big or Small—Why do we care? *Narrative Inquiry, 16*, 139–147.

Bamberg, M. (Ed.). (2007). *Narrative: State of the Art*. Amsterdam: John Benjamins.

Bamberg, M., & Andrews, M. (Eds.). (2004). *Considering Counter-Narratives: Narrating, Resisting, Making Sense*. Amsterdam: John Benjamins.

Bartlett, F. (1995). *Remembering: A Study in Experimental and Social Psychology* Cambridge: Cambridge University Press. (Originally 1932).

Birkerts, S. (2008). *The Art of Time in Memoir: Then, Again*. St. Paul, MN: Graywolf Press.

Bonnefoy, Y. (1989). *The Act and the Place of Poetry*. Chicago: The University of Chicago Press.

Brockmeier, J. (1997). Autobiography, narrative, and the Freudian concept of life history. *Philosophy, Psychiatry, & Psychology, 4,* 175–199.

Brockmeier, J. (2000). Autobiographical time. *Narrative Inquiry, 10,* 51–73.

Brockmeier, J. (2001). From the beginning to the end: Retrospective teleology in Autobiography. In J. Brockmeier & D. Carbaugh (Eds.), *Narrative and Identity: Studies in Autobiography, Self, and Culture* (pp. 246–280). Amsterdam: John Benjamins.

Brockmeier, J. (Ed.). (2002). Special volume on "Narrative and Cultural Memory. *Culture and Psychology, 8.*

Brockmeier, J., & Carbaugh, D. (Eds.). (2001). *Narrative and Identity: Studies in Autobiography, Self and Culture.* Amsterdam: John Benjamins.

Brooks, P. (1985). *Reading for the Plot: Design and Intention in Narrative.* Ithaca, NY: Cornell University Press.

Bruner, J. (1990). *Acts of Meaning.* Cambridge, MA: Harvard University Press.

Bruner, J. (2003). *Making Stories: Law, Literature, Life.* Cambridge, MA: Harvard University Press.

Butler, J. (2005). *Giving an Account of Oneself.* New York: Fordham University Press.

Carr, D. (1986). *Time, Narrative, and History.* Bloomingon: Indiana University Press.

Charmé, S.L. (1984). *Meaning and Myth in the Study of Lives.* Philadelphia: University of Pennsylvania Press.

Clandinin, J. (Ed.). (2006). *Handbook of Narrative Inquiry: Mapping a Methodology.* Beverly Hills, CA: Sage.

Conway, J.K. (1989). *The Road from Coorain.* New York: Alfred A. Knopf.

Daiute, C. & Lightfoot, C. (Eds.). (2003). *Narrative Analysis: Studying the Development of Individuals in Society.* Beverly Hills, CA: Sage.

Dillard, A. (1987). To fashion a text. In W. Zinsser (Ed.), *Inventing the Truth: The Art and Craft of Memoir* (pp. 55–76). Boston: Houghton Mifflin.

Dilthey, W. (1976). "The construction of the historical world in the human studies. In H.P. Rickman (Ed.), *Dilthey: Selected Writings.* Cambridge: Cambridge University Press. (Originally published 1910)

Eakin, P.J. (2008). *Living Autobiographically: How We Create Identity in Narrative.* Ithaca, NY:Cornell University Press.

Eliade, M. (1954). *The Myth of the Eternal Return: Or, Cosmos and History.* Princeton, NJ: Princeton University Press.

Erikson, E.H. (1994). *Identity and the Life Cycle.* New York: W.W. Norton.

Fentress, J., & Wickham, C. (1992). *Social Memory.* London, UK: Blackwell.

Fineman, G., McVay, T., & Flanagan, O. (Eds.). (2003). *Narrative and Consciousness: Literature, Psychology, and the Brain.* New York: Oxford University Press.

Fischoff, B. (1975). Hindsight ≠ foresight: The effect of outcome knowledge on judgment under uncertainty. *Journal of Experimental Psychology: Human Perception and Performance, 104,* 288–299.

Fivush, R., & Hayden, C.A. (Eds.). (2003). *Autobiographical Memory and the Construction of a Narrative Self: Developmental and Cultural Perspectives.* Hillsdale, NJ: Lawrence Erlbaum.

Flanagan, O. (1996). *Self Expressions: Mind, Morals, and the Meaning of Life* Oxford: Oxford University Press.

Freeman, M. (1984). History, narrative, and life-span developmental knowledge. *Human Development, 27,* 1–19.

Freeman, M. (1985). Psychoanalytic narration and the problem of historical knowledge. *Psychoanalysis and Contemporary Thought, 8,* 133–182.

Freeman, M. (1991). Rewriting the self: Development as moral practice. In M.B. Tappan & M.J. Packer (Eds.), *Narrative Approaches to Moral Development. New Directions for Child Development, 54,* 83–101.

Freeman, M. (1993). *Rewriting the Self: History, Memory, Narrative.* London: Routledge.

Freeman, M. (1994). *Finding the Muse: A Sociopsychological Inquiry into the Conditions of Artistic Creativity.* Cambridge: Cambridge University Press.

Freeman, M. (1997a). Why narrative? Hermeneutics, historical understanding, and the significance of stories. *Journal of Narrative and Life History, 7,* 169–176.

Freeman, M. (1997b). Death, narrative integrity, and the radical challenge of self-understanding: A reading of Tolstoy's *Death of Ivan Ilych. Ageing and Society, 17,* 373–398.

Freeman, M. (1998). Mythical time, historical time, and the narrative fabric of the self. *Narrative Inquiry, 8,* 27–50.

Freeman, M. (1999). Culture, narrative, and the poetic construction of selfhood. *Journal of Constructivist Psychology, 12,* 99–116.

Freeman, M. (2000a). When the story's over: Narrative foreclosure and the possibility of self-renewal. In M. Andrews, S.D. Sclater, C. Squire, and A. Treacher (Eds.), *Lines of Narrative: Psychosocial Perspectives* (pp. 81–91). London: Routledge.

Freeman, M. (2000b). Modernists at heart? Postmodern artistic breakdowns and the question of identity. In D. Fee (Ed.), *Pathology and the Postmodern: Mental Illness as Discourse and Experience* (pp. 116–140). Beverly Hills, CA: Sage.

Freeman, M. (2001). Tradition und Erinnerung des Selbst und der Kultur (Tradition and memory in self and culture). In H. Welzer (Ed.), *Das Soziale Gedächtnis: Geschichte, Erinnerung, Tradierung* (*Social Memory: History, Remembrance, Tradition*) (pp. 25–40). Hamburg: Hamburger Edition.

Freeman, M. (2002a). Charting the narrative unconscious: Cultural memory and the challenge of autobiography. *Narrative Inquiry, 12,* 193–211.

Freeman, M. (2002b). The burden of truth: Psychoanalytic *poiesis* and narrative understanding. In W. Patterson (Ed.), *Strategic Narrative: New Perspectives on the Power of Personal and Cultural Stories* (pp. 9–27). Lanham, MD: Lexington Books.

Freeman, M. (2002c). The presence of what is missing: Memory, poetry, and the ride home. In R.J. Pellegrini & T.R. Sarbin (Eds.), *Between Fathers and Sons: Critical Incident Narratives in the Development of Men's Lives* (pp. 165–176). Binghamton, NY: Haworth.

Freeman, M. (2003a). Too late: The temporality of memory and the challenge of moral life. *Journal fur Psychologie, 11,* 54–74.

Freeman, M. (2003b). Rethinking the fictive, reclaiming the real: Autobiography, narrative time, and the burden of truth. In G. Fireman, T. McVay, & O. Flanagan (Eds.), *Narrative and Consciousness: Literature, Psychology, and the Brain* (pp. 115–128). New York: Oxford University Press.

Freeman, M. (2006). Life "on holiday"? In defense of big stories. *Narrative Inquiry, 16,* 131–138.

Freeman, M. (2007). Narrative and relation: The place of the Other in the story of the self. In R. Josselson, A. Lieblich, & D. McAdams (Eds.), *The Meaning of Others: Narrative Studies of Relationships* (pp. 11–19). Washington, DC: APA Books.

Freeman, M., & Brockmeier, J. (2001). Narrative integrity: Autobiographical identity and the meaning of the "good life." In J. Brockmeier & D. Carbaugh (Eds.), *Narrative and Identity: Studies in Autobiography, Self and Culture* (pp. 75–99). Amsterdam: John Benjamins.

Freeman, M., & Robinson R. (1990). The development within: An alternative approach to the study of lives. *New Ideas in Psychology, 8,* 53–72.

Freud, S. (1958). Remembering, repeating, and working-through. *Standard Edition XII* (pp. 147–156). London: Hogarth. (Originally 1914)

Freud, S. (1962). Further remarks on the neuro-psychoses of defense. *Standard Edition III.* London: Hogarth. (Originally 1896)

Freud, S. (1966). Project for a scientific psychology. *Standard Edition 1.* London: Hogarth. (Originally 1895)

Frey, J. (2005). *A Million Little Pieces.* New York: Anchor.

Gadamer, H.-G. (1975). *Truth and Method.* New York: Crossroad.

Gadamer, H.-G. (1976). *Philosophical Hermeneutics.* Berkeley, CA: University of California Press.

Gantt, E.E., & Williams, R.N. (Eds.). (2002). *Psychology for the Other: Levinas, Ethics and the Practice of Psychology.* Pittsburgh, PA: Duquesne University Press.

Gazzaniga, M.S. (1998). *The Mind's Past.* Berkeley, CA: University of California Press.

Georgakopoulou, A. (2006). Thinking big with small stories in narrative and identity analysis. *Narrative Inquiry, 16,* 129–137.

Gordon, E.F. (2003). Book of days. *American Scholar, 72,* 17–32.

Gusdorf, G. (1980). Conditions and limits of autobiography. In J. Olney (Ed.), *Autobiography: Essays Theoretical and Critical* (pp. 28–48). Princeton, NJ: Princeton University Press.

Hacking, I. (1995). *Rewriting the Soul: Multiple Personality and the Sciences Of Memory.* Princeton, NJ: Princeton University Press.

Halbwachs, M. (1992). *On Collective Memory.* Chicago: The University of Chicago Press.

Hampl, P. (1999). *I Could Tell You Stories: Sojourns in the Land of Memory.* New York: W.W. Norton.

Hawkins, S.A., & Hastie R. (1990). Hindsight: Biased judgments of past events after the outcomes are known. *Psychological Bulletin, 107,* 311–327.

Heaney, S. (1995). *The Redress of Poetry*. New York: The Noonday Press.

Heidegger, M. (1962). *Being and Time*. New York: Harper & Row. (Originally published 1927)

Heidegger, M. (1971). *Poetry, Language, Thought*. New York: Harper Colophon.

Hertwig, R., Fanselow, C., & Hoffrage, U. (2003). Hindsight bias: How knowledge and heuristics affect our reconstruction of the past. *Memory, 11* (4/5), 357–377.

Hoerl, C., & McCormack, T. (Eds.). (2001). *Time and Memory: Issues in Philosophy and Psychology*. Oxford: Clarendon Press.

Hoffman, E. (2004). *After Such Knowledge: Memory, History, and the Legacy of the Holocaust*. New York: Public Affairs.

Hoffrage, U., & Pohl, R.F. (2003). Research on hindsight bias: A rich past, a productive present, and a challenging future. *Memory, 11* (4/5), 329–345.

Holstein, J.A., & Gubrium, J.B. (2000). *The Self We Live By: Narrative Identity in a Postmodern World*. New York: Oxford University Press.

James, W. (1985). *The Varieties of Religious Experience*. New York: Penguin. (Originally 1902)

Jauss, H.R. (1989). *Question and Answer: Forms of Dialogic Understanding*. Minneapolis, MN: University of Minnesota Press.

Josselson, R. (2004). The hermeneutics of faith and the hermeneutics of suspicion. *Narrative Inquiry, 14*, 1–28.

Josselson, R., Lieblich, A., & McAdams, D. (Eds.). (2007). *The Meaning of Others: Narrative Studies of Relationships*. Washington, DC: APA Books.

Kearney, R. (2001). *On Stories*. London: Routledge.

Kerby, A.P. (1991). *Narrative and the Self*. Bloomington: Indiana University Press.

Kermode, F. (1967). *The Sense of an Ending*. Oxford: Oxford University Press.

Kermode, F. (1978). *The Genesis of Secrecy: On the Interpretation of Narrative*. Cambridge, MA: Harvard University Press.

King, N. (2000). *Memory, Narrative, Identity: Remembering the Self*. Edinburgh: Edinburgh University Press.

Lear, J. (1998). *Open-Minded: Working Out the Logic of the Soul*. Cambridge, MA: Harvard University Press.

Leiris, M. (1984). *Manhood: A Journey from Childhood into the Fierce Order of Virility*. Chicago: University of Chicago Press. (Originally 1939)

Levi, P. (1989). *The Drowned and the Saved*. New York: Vintage International.

Levi, P. (1995). *The Reawakening*. Touchstone.

Levinas, E. (1985). *Ethics and Infinity*. Pittsburgh, PA: Duquesne University Press.

Levinas, E. (1994). *Outside the Subject*. Palo Alto, CA: Stanford University Press.

Levinas, E. (1996). Substitution. In Peperzak, A.T., Critchley, S. & Bernasconi, R. (Eds.), *Emmanuel Levinas: Basic Philosophical Writings* (pp. 80–95). Bloomington: Indiana University Press.

Levinas, E. (1999). *Alterity and Transcendence*. New York: Columbia University Press.

Lieblich, A., McAdams, D.P., & Josselson, R. (Eds.). (2004). *Healing Plots: The Narrative Basis of Psychotherapy.* Washington, DC: American Psychological Association.

Lloyd, G. (1993). *Being in Time: Selves and Narrators in Philosophy and Literature.* London: Routledge.

Ludwig, A. (1997). *How Do We Know Who We Are? A Biography of the Self.* Oxford: Oxford University Press.

Lukacher, N. (1986). *Primal Scenes: Literature, Philosophy, Psychoanalysis.* Ithaca, NY: Cornell University Press.

MacIntyre, A. (1981). *After Virtue: A Study in Moral Theory.* Notre Dame, IN: University of Notre Dame Press.

Marcel, G. (1950). *The Mystery of Being, Vol. 1: Reflection and Mystery.* Chicago: Henry Regnery Co.

McAdams, D. (1997). *The Stories We Live By: Personal Myths and the Making of the Self.* New York: Guilford.

McAdams, D.P. (2005). *The Redemptive Self: Stories Americans Live By.* New York: Oxford University Press.

McAdams, D.P., Josselson, R., & Lieblich, A. (Eds.). (2001). *Turns in the Road: Narrative Studies of Lives in Transition.* Washington, DC: American Psychological Association.

McAdams, D.P., Josselson, R., & Lieblich, A. (Eds.). (2006). *Identity and Story: Creating Self in Narrative.* Washington, DC: American Psychological Association.

McCarthy, M. (1963). *Memories of a Catholic Girlhood.* New York: Berkley Publishing Co.

Messer, S.B., Sass, L.A., & Woolfolks, R.L. (Eds.). (1988). *Hermeneutics and Psychological Theory.* New Brunswick, NJ: Rutgers University Press.

Milosz, C. (1981). *Native Realm: A Search for Self-Definition.* Berkeley, CA: University of California Press.

Most, G.W. (1989). The stranger's stratagem: Self-disclosure and self-sufficiency in Greek culture. *Journal of Hellenic Studies, CIX,* 114–133.

Muldoon, M.S. (2006). *Tricks of Time: Bergson, Merleau-Ponty and Ricoeur in Search of Time, Self and Meaning.* Pittsburgh, PA: Duquesne University Press.

Murdoch, I. (1970). *The Sovereignty of Good.* London: Routledge.

Murdoch, I. (1993). *Metaphysics as a Guide to Morals.* London: Penguin.

Nehamas, A. (1985). *Nietzsche: Life as Literature.* Cambridge, MA: Harvard University Press.

Nietzsche, F.W. (1966). *Beyond Good and Evil.* New York: Vintage. (Originally 1886)

Nietzsche, F.W. (1968). *The Will to Power.* New York: Vintage. (Originally 1888)

Nietzsche, F.W. (1974). *The Gay Science.* New York: Vintage. (Originally 1887)

Olney, J. (2000). *Memory and Narrative: The Weave of Life-Writing.* Chicago: University of Chicago Press.

Packer, M.J., & Addison, R.B. (Eds.). (1989). *Entering the Circle: Hermeneutic Investigation in Psychology.* Albany, NY: SUNY Press.

Patterson, W. (Ed.). (2002). *Strategic Narrative: New Perspectives on the Power of Personal and Cultural Stories.* Lanham, MD: Lexington Books.

Plato. (2003). *The Republic.* New York: Penguin.

Polkinghorne, D. (1988). *Narrative Knowing and the Human Sciences.* Albany, NY: SUNY Press.

Rabinow, P., & Sullivan, W.M. (Eds.). (1979). *Interpretive Social Science: A Reader.* Berkeley, CA: University of California Press.

Rabinow, P. & Sullivan, W.M. (Eds.). (1987). *Interpretive Social Science: A Second Look.* Berkeley, CA: University of California Press.

Ricoeur, P. (1970). *Freud and Philosophy: An Essay on Interpretation.* New Haven, CT: Yale University of Press.

Ricoeur, P. (1974). *The Conflict of Interpretations.* Evanston, IL: Northwestern University Press.

Ricoeur, P. (1976). *Interpretation Theory: Discourse and the Surplus of Meaning.* Fort Worth: Texas Christian University Press.

Ricoeur, P. (1981a). *Hermeneutics and the Human Sciences.* Cambridge, UK: Cambridge University Press.

Ricoeur, P. (1981b). Narrative time. In W.J.T. Mitchell (Ed.), *On Narrative* (pp. 165–186). Chicago: University of Chicago Press.

Ricoeur, P. (1984). *Time and Narrative,* Vol. 1. Chicago: University of Chicago Press.

Ricoeur, P. (1985). *Time and Narrative,* Vol. 2. Chicago: University of Chicago Press.

Ricoeur, P. (1988). *Time and Narrative, Vol. 3.* Chicago: University of Chicago Press.

Ricoeur, P. (1991). Life in quest of narrative. In D. Wood (Ed.), *On Paul Ricoeur: Narrative and Interpretation* (pp. 20–33). London: Routledge.

Ricoeur, P. (1992). *Oneself as Another.* Chicago: University of Chicago Press.

Ricoeur, P. (2006). *Memory, History, Forgetting.* Chicago: University of Chicago Press.

Riessman, C.K. (2007). *Narrative Methods for the Human Sciences.* Beverly Hills, CA: Sage.

Ross, B.M. (1991). *Remembering the Personal Past.* Oxford University Press.

Ross, B.M., & Wilson, A.E. (2000). Constructing and appraising past selves. In D.L. Schacter & E. Scarry (Eds.). (2001). *Memory, Brain, and Belief* (pp. 231–258). Cambridge, MA: Harvard University Press.

Roth, P. (1988). *The Facts.* New York: Farrar, Straus, & Giroux.

Sampson, E.E. (1993). *Celebrating the Other: A Dialogical Account of Human Nature.* Boulder, CO: Westfield Press.

Sarbin, T.R. (1986). *Narrative Psychology: The Storied Nature of Human Conduct.* New York: Praeger.

Sartwell, C. (2000). *End of Story: Toward the Annihilation of Language and History.* Albany, NY: SUNY.

Schachtel, E. (1959). *Metamorphosis: On the Conflict of Human Development and the Psychology of Creativity.* New York: Basic Books.

Schacter, D.L. (1995). Memory distortion: History and current status. In D.L. Schacter (Ed.), *Memory Distortion: How Minds, Brains, and Societies Reconstruct the Past* (pp.1–43). Cambridge, MA: Harvard University Press.

Schacter, D.L. (1996). *Searching for Memory: The Brain, The Mind, and the Past.* New York: Basic Books.

Schacter, D.L. (2001). *The Seven Sins of Memory (How the Mind Forgets and Remembers).* Boston, MA: Houghton Mifflin Company.

Schacter, D.L., & Scarry, E. (2000). *Memory, Brain, and Belief.* Cambridge, MA: Harvard University Press.

Shils, E.A. (1981). *Tradition.* Chicago: University of Chicago Press.

Shweder, R.A. & Bourne, E.J. (1984). Does the concept of the person vary cross-culturally? In R.A. Shweder & R.A. LeVine (Eds.), Culture Theory: Essays on Mind, Self, and Emotion (pp. 158–199). Cambridge: Cambridge University Press.

Slater, L. (2000). *Lying: A Metaphorical Memoir.* New York: Penguin Books.

Smith, P. (1988). *Discerning the Subject.* Minneapolis: University of Minnesota Press.

Sontag, S. (2003). *Regarding the Pain of Others.* New York: Farrar, Straus and Giroux.

Spence, D.P. (1982). *Narrative Truth and Historical Truth.* New York: W.W. Norton.

Stern, D. (2004). *The Present Moment in Psychotherapy and Everyday Life.* New York: W.W. Norton & Company.

Taylor, C. (1989). *Sources of the Self.* Cambridge, MA: Harvard University Press.;

Taylor, C. (1991). *The Ethics of Authenticity.* Cambridge, MA: Harvard University Press.

Tolle, E. (2004). *The Power of Now: A Guide to Spiritual Enlightenment.* New World Library.

Tolstoy, L. (1960). *The Death of Ivan Ilych and Other Stories.* New York: New American Library. (Originally 1886)

Updike, J. (1989). *Self-Consciousness.* New York: Alfred A. Knopf.

Vendler, H. (1995). *Soul Says.* Cambridge, MA: Harvard University Press.

Vernant, J.-P. (Ed.) (1995). The Greeks. Chicago, IL: University of Chicago Press.

Weil, S. (1997). *Gravity and Grace.* London: Routledge. (Originally published 1952)

Weintraub, K. (1978). *The Value of the Individual: Self and Circumstance in Autobiography.* Chicago: University of Chicago Press.

White, H. (1978). *Tropics of Discourse.* Baltimore, MD: Johns Hopkins University Press.

White, H. (1990). *The Content of the Form: Narrative Discourse and Historical Representation.* Baltimore: Johns Hopkins University Press.

Zerubavel, E. (2004). *Time Maps: Collective Memory and the Social Shape of the Past.* Chicago: University of Chicago Press.

INDEX